D1625313

Love Leads is a must-read for all those in a position of leadership. My friend Dr. Steve Greene challenges readers to lead those entrusted to them with truth and love. This book will change the way you lead and love!

—JOHN BEVERE
AUTHOR AND MINISTER
MESSENGER INTERNATIONAL

Messenger International Dr. Steve Greene has a gift of encouragement that lifts leaders into greater confidence and productivity—regardless of the task. His insights will inspire and challenge you to lead with excellence. I highly recommend this book.

—DR. RICE BROOCKS
AUTHOR, *GOD'S NOT DEAD*

Leaders and potential leaders should read this book. Dr. Greene's successful leadership experience in business, ministry, and academia provides a vantage point few possess. By identifying love as the key component of leadership, this book provides a foundation for the long-term success of leaders and followers. Readers will find the book applicable to leadership in ministry, business, and families. The well-written, jargon-free book is easy to read, biblically sound, and spiritually deep.

—JAMES RUSSELL, PhD
PROFESSOR OF ECONOMICS AND CHAIR OF THE
UNDERGRADUATE COLLEGE OF BUSINESS,
ORAL ROBERTS UNIVERSITY

Dr. Steve Greene's extraordinary leadership principles are summed up in one word: *love*. In reading his book, I'm reminded afresh that "knowledge puffs up, but love edifies" (1 Cor. 8:1, NKJV). I deeply respect and appreciate this book and the man who wrote it!

His book on leadership is rooted in the second greatest commandment: "Love your neighbor as yourself" (Matt. 22:39, NKJV; see also verses 37–38, 40.) This refreshing take on leadership emphasizes the fact that love will indeed build a strong team united in vision, mission, and camaraderie. Dr. Greene draws a wealth of insights about leadership from his study of the Bible, making this an exceptional go-to resource for aspiring and seasoned leaders alike.

—RON LEWIS
SENIOR MINISTER, EVERY NATION CHURCH, NEW YORK CITY, AND KING'S PARK INTERNATIONAL CHURCH, DURHAM, NORTH CAROLINA

Dr. Greene is an amazing leader. He sees people for who they can be and calls it out of them. Much of who I am, personally and professionally, is a testament to that. People naturally gravitate toward him. His presence encourages everyone he encounters to come up higher. Dr. Greene possesses the finest ability to apply leadership strategy. What's more, the anointing on him in this capacity is significant; the Spirit undoubtedly speaks and attracts through him. *Love Leads* is a fantastic work that I've seen Dr. Greene live out as long as

I've known him as a professor, pastor, mentor, business leader, and friend.

—ROBERT BARBOSA, MBA
REGIONAL ACCOUNT MANAGER, FRITO-LAY

I consider my relationship with Dr. Greene to be one of my life's greatest blessings. Since meeting Dr. Greene eight years ago, I've known him as a dean, professor, pastor, mentor, and friend. So much of who I've grown to be as a lifelong student, believer, wife, and professional is the result of Dr. Greene's ability to lead in love—and I know countless others who can say the same. Dr. Greene sees people not according to what they do but rather according to the fullness of their hearts—he sees them as Christ sees them. *Love Leads* is a beautifully written book about just this.

—AMANDA BARBOSA, MBA
ADVERTISING MANAGER, TACO BELL

The Spiritual Connection
Between Your Relationships
and Productivity

LOVE ~~STRENGTH~~ LEADS

DR. STEVE GREENE

CHARISMA
HOUSE

LOVE LEADS by Dr. Steve Greene
Published by Charisma House
Charisma Media/Charisma House Book Group
600 Rinehart Road
Lake Mary, Florida 32746
www.charismahouse.com

Cover design by Lisa Rae McClure
Design Director: Justin Evans

Visit the author's websites at drstevegreene.com and loveleadsbook.com.

Library of Congress Cataloging-in-Publication Data:
An application to register this book for cataloging has been submitted to the Library of Congress.
International Standard Book Number: 978-1-62998-706-4
E-book ISBN: 978-1-62998-707-1

This publication is translated in Spanish under the title *El amor lidera*, copyright © 2017 by Dr. Steve Greene, published by Casa Creación, a Charisma Media company. All rights reserved.

17 18 19 20 21 — 9 8 7 6 5 4 3 2 1
Printed in the United States of America

To my wife, Anette.

You've always demonstrated the love of a leader in our home. Thank you for loving me through every exciting adventure.

CONTENTS

ACKNOWLEDGMENTS

Wʜᴇɴ ᴀʀᴇ ʏᴏᴜ going to write a book?" I've deflected this question for at least the last thirty years. My books live in the lives of all the students I've had the privilege of teaching throughout my career. I've loved my students and taught with the single motivation of preparing them for a life as a spiritual leader in the marketplace. I pray that their contributions to the kingdom will fill thousands of books.

I'm deeply grateful to Joy Strang for encouraging me to write this book. She spoke words of life over me and this book throughout my writing journey. Thanks to Steve Strang for trusting me to lead his media group while I wrote at some very odd hours. Thank you, Steve and Joy, for the opportunity to work with you.

Thanks to our Charisma House publisher, Marcos Perez, and his outstanding team for agreeing to publish this book. Thank you, Debbie Marrie, for grace and understanding.

How does one begin to thank an editor? Adrienne

Gaines is an outstanding editor, and I was privileged to work with her on this book. The good news for readers is that I listened to her, and she greatly improved the readability of this book. Along the way she taught me about writing, but she also encouraged me to be confident and to believe in the words God was giving me. Thank you, Adrienne. You blessed me with your gifts.

Thank you to Mark Rutland for demonstrating servant leadership to me during our time together at Oral Roberts University. I would need another book to fully describe all that you and Alison have meant to me.

Along the way I've worked with many leaders. I have learned from each of you. Thank you.

To Jim and Sophia Russell, thank you for modeling leadership in our church. I was honored to serve with you. You both hear from the Lord. He continues to bless you with gold dust.

Jennifer LeClaire is the most prolific and highest-quality writer I have ever worked with. She writes in the Spirit. Her words flow directly from heaven. Thank you for your help and strong support. Thank you for praying for me on those days when I wanted to stop writing. Please maintain the prophetic gift within you. I'm blessed by you every day.

Thank you to my Lois, Opal Hamilton, who prayed for me to find the Lord, and to Sheree Carter for leading me to Jesus. And to my sister, Debbie, who walks daily to be more like Him, thank you for never giving up on me. I love you.

Thank you to my children, Kimberly and Landon, who patiently waited for me to learn to lead. Live your lives with love. Thanks also to my grandchildren—Kaitlin, Treyton, and Kolby—who love so perfectly. Do your homework! Always love learning.

Most of all, thank You, Jesus, for sending the Comforter to fill me and lead the writing of this book.

FOREWORD

I FIRST BECAME THE "senior pastor" of a church at the ripe old age of twenty-two. The title implied several things, none of which were true. The very phrase seems to hint there were others on the staff whom I led as their "senior." Not only were there no other pastors on staff; there were no other employees of any kind, and I myself was part time. In addition, the word *senior* might also speak of age. In fact, there were hardly any members younger than I was, and my wife was the youngest person in the young adults Sunday school class.

The last faint hope for real meaning in the phrase, that as a pastor I was "senior" to the laity in Bible knowledge or ministry experience, was hope against hope. I blush to think of what and how I preached in those salad days of yore. I may not have taught anyone anything, but much of what I learned at that little country church has helped me for fifty years of leadership in multiple churches and two universities.

An elderly farmer, a man "senior" to me in every way, told me a story I've never forgotten. It seems that many years before, a tree salesman had come through the territory selling fruit trees. By the time I arrived in the area, the evidence of his salesmanship lined driveways and shaded backyards all across the county.

It seems the salesman sold the trees at a modest price, a price so low, in fact, that he would not guarantee the trees unless the purchaser would also buy and use a bag of secret powder. Then and only then were the trees guaranteed.

Not everyone, the old man told me, would spring for the secret potion. Many who refused that extra cost lost their trees in the very first year. The trees of virtually everyone who bought the secret powder thrived. The powder was to be sprinkled into a gallon bucket of water and poured around the roots of the tree three times a day. Those who bought the powder and followed the directions were amazed at the results.

The old man pointed to a peach tree in his side yard that was lush with fruit. "That's one right there. I poured that secret powder on that one, and look at it. That tree is old. Older 'n you, I reckon. And just look at it. Looks like that powder was almost magical, don't it?"

"I suppose so," I said. "What do you think was in it?"

"Oh, I know exactly what was in it. After I had poured

probably a hundred buckets of water around my trees, I tasted that there powder. You know what was in it?"

"What?"

"Cinnamon. Weren't nothing but plain cinnamon. What do you think of that?"

I was dubious, to say the least, but I did not want to hurt his feelings. "Well, I don't know what to think. I didn't know cinnamon would help trees grow."

"It didn't," he said. "Didn't do one blessed thing."

"I don't get it," I said. "If it didn't help, why did the tree do better?"

"It was the water!" He laughed and slapped his straw hat against his thigh. "The secret powder was just a trick to get us to water them trees. It was all that water that was the secret ingredient."

I thought of that story when I read Dr. Greene's book on leadership. There are many things to learn about leadership and plenty worth teaching. Dr. Greene has found the secret ingredient, the one that will make leadership grow and thrive rather than wither and die. This book is about one thing: the secret powder that makes leadership work.

—DR. MARK RUTLAND
FOUNDER AND PRESIDENT, GLOBAL SERVANTS
BEST-SELLING AUTHOR, *ReLaunch*

Chapter 1

THE CASE FOR LOVE

I F GOD IS love and we have not love, how then shall we lead?

It's not difficult to find books, blogs, or videos on the topic of leadership today. It seems everyone has an opinion about how leaders should lead. Leaders meet about it. Followers weigh in on it. Scholars opine about it. Yet it seems we cry out for leaders to emerge.

The synthesis of leadership resources is usually a list of characteristics describing what effective leaders do or don't do. The book in your hands, however, is focused on one powerful component of leadership that is rarely discussed. Effective leaders love the people they lead.

Love makes the difference.

The apostle Paul said it best in 1 Corinthians: "If I have all faith, so that I could remove mountains, and have not love, I am nothing" (1 Cor. 13:2). Of course most leaders would be quick to agree that it's much easier to move a mountain than it is to move people.

People need love more today than ever before, but

business leaders have been too busy to love their teams. There always seems to be higher priorities than taking time to show compassion. It's so easy to bark a command and then expect joyful compliance. Sometimes all that is needed to demonstrate love is a kinder tone and better language when asking for a job to be completed.

A story is often told about a young boy whose mother orders him every morning to take a bucket to the well and fill it with water. Each day the boy replies, "I will not do it!" But then he grabs the bucket handle and rushes away to pump the water. The boy resented the command but in his own way recognized the need for water. He was willing to respond to the need to supply water but was not willing to obey the cold command to go fetch it.

> **Sometimes all that is needed to demonstrate love is a kinder tone and better language when asking for a job to be completed.**

Hidden in this story is an essential need of workers—and probably humanity—for organizational needs to be presented in a loving manner. When situations develop in an organization, they must lead to conversations. Simply to show the worker the required solution is to keep that person in a place of subordination or servility. To move beyond that status, a worker must hear that clear and present need expressed in love. He must see that he is more than a cog in the organization's wheel; he must know that he matters.

Love has often been viewed as a weakness in a leader. The belief exists that love is in some way a soft skill and leaders should be tough as nails and yell a lot. Soft skills don't seem to be in demand in the marketplace. Organizations crave strong leadership.

Can a strong leader have a soft style?

Love certainly was not a valued leadership quality during the Industrial Revolution when management pioneer Frederick Taylor was shaping what would become the prevailing managing style. Taylor taught that leaders must manage workers with the proverbial carrot and stick. The Taylor approach was to threaten the workers' security. The mantra echoed: "Work faster and better, or we will find someone who can." Taylor felt that workers were more productive when they feared the loss of employment.

I suggest that "love leaders" are better than "stick leaders." Love pulls a team forward, while a stick pushes a team to a breaking point. It is my belief that a work team will produce better results when loved than when "sticked."

Having said that, let me be clear: this book is not

intended to be an academic primer on leadership in the workplace. I don't offer pages of statistics or empirical evidence that love increases worker productivity. I offer spiritual insight into how leaders can love more, develop better relationships, and achieve improved productivity.

The typical case studies presented in leadership books are replaced in this book by examples of how leaders love as presented in the Bible. We will study how various biblical figures loved, and then I will suggest how we may apply leadership principles from Scripture to today's marketplace.

As leaders our goal is to meet certain profit or productivity metrics. As followers of Christ our mandate is to model the character of Jesus in all we do. The two are not mutually exclusive. Love should never be abandoned in pursuit of the bottom line. When a Pharisee asked what the greatest commandment was, Jesus said, "'You shall love the Lord your God with all your heart, and with all your soul, and with all your mind.' This is the first and great commandment. And the second is like it: 'You shall love your neighbor as yourself.' On these two commandments hang all the Law and the Prophets" (Matt. 22:37–40). Everything we do—whether at work, at home, or in our day-to-day interactions—should be done in love. Our leadership is no exception.

The love we are called to model isn't the kind you see

in movies or read about in books. We are not to love our teams as Romeo loved Juliet or even as Dr. Watson loved his friend Sherlock Holmes. Romantic feelings fade, and friends change. The love we are to model to our teams, the kind of love that breeds influence, is the love God has shown us.

Love motivates everything God says and does—including His wise leadership. God sees us through the eyes of Christ—and He sees even the lost soul's potential if he will surrender to His love. When we fall short of His glory, God doesn't shame us and guilt us; He teaches and coaches. His discipline and correction in our lives are rooted in His perfect love for us (Heb. 12:6).

"God so loved" that He made a plan. He gave us His Son, thus demonstrating that giving is loving. In His magnificent leadership God shows Himself to be the consummate cheerful giver. He gives all He has. He's a sacrificial giver, a life giver, a reward giver. God is the greatest giver of all. Indeed, we can't out-give God—but we can try to love people as He does.

Love-Driven Leadership Is Intentional

We know love is more about action than emotion. We do things for people we care about. Warm and fuzzy feelings are not a necessary ingredient. Clear intentions are most necessary for action to occur. Great leaders don't love by accident. Love-driven leadership is intentional.

When we give direction to a work team, we show love by leading the action from the front of the pack. In doing this, we demonstrate good technique long before we evaluate the performance of others. When leaders demonstrate how to do a thing in the right way, love is the stimulant. When we care about people, we care about their success. There is no demonstration of love in leaders who claim, "It would have been easier and faster if I had just done it myself."

The language of a leader goes a long way toward establishing a loving, nurturing work environment. In later chapters I will provide clear direction on the language of leaders in any environment, as the heart of a leader is often revealed in the words used to lead a team. Here I simply want to remind you that new languages can be learned. Vocabulary can be changed and improved. Words of death can be replaced with words of life and love.

This does not mean we avoid speaking the truth. The apostle Paul admonished the Ephesians to speak the truth in love so the church could grow. Loving leadership doesn't deny the truth, but it uses truth telling to bring growth, not pain.

Often it is our words that make the biggest difference

to those we lead. Too many leaders learn too late that their words have not caused love to grow.

> **Loving leadership doesn't deny the truth, but it uses truth telling to bring growth, not pain.**

The language of love is needed beyond the office. The words that reverberate in a home frequently are the ones that are careless and hurtful. A bad day in the home has more consequences than a bad day at the office. I once heard someone say: "Home is where I don't have to guard my words and actions. My home is my castle, and I don't have to be on guard all the time." I believe the opposite is true.

We cannot relax our intentional display of love in our homes. It seems unreasonable to me to think that I clearly demonstrate love at the office but keep the people at home guessing about my feelings. I would never even consider "biting off the head" of someone at work. But at home if I think I can growl without consequence, I will surely harvest the fruit of my behavior— very quickly. No one in my home, for even a brief moment, should doubt the depth of my love as a leader.

Highly effective leaders lead well in every environment, whether at home, in the workplace, at church, or in personal relationships. Although this book focuses mostly on organizational leadership, these principles can—and should—be applied to all areas of life. Indeed, leaders who leave a legacy of love are known for their successful leadership in the home, at work, and in their multitude of relationships.

Love-Driven Leadership
Seeks Out Potential

God has a plan for every person we will ever lead. I believe it is my responsibility to lead people to ful-fill God's plan. God's plan is my potential. Leaders must love a team into their potential. My purpose as a leader is to lead my team into God's purpose. Perhaps we could define bad leadership as leading people away from God. A loving leader couldn't do that.

> **Highly effective leaders lead well in every environment, whether at home, in the workplace, at church, or in personal relationships.**

Technically speaking, *potential* means "existing in possibility: capable of development into actuality," according to Merriam-Webster's dictionary.[1] Potential is what's possible but not always what's present-tense reality.

For many the word *potential* is a burden. Perhaps

the pressure comes from being born into a successful family. Or maybe the evidence of talent at a very young age brings high expectations. I suppose that from baby nurseries to graduation stages the most noted thought among observers is the presence of unlimited potential.

After thirty-plus years of working with college students, I've concluded there are very few markers for true potential. Leaders see potential in almost everyone they work with. I remember a pastor told me once: "See that guy? He's thirty-eight and has lots of potential. What that really means is, he ain't done nothing yet."

It seems to me there's a lot of truth in that statement. The real difference in people is the realization of potential. I think the fulfillment of potential has a lot to do with a person's spiritual condition. There are certainly successful and talented heathens. And there are those who have moved away from God's presence who are doing well in their own eyes. But human potential is limited without God.

What is the spiritual definition of *potential*? Paul may have said it best: "to know Him, and the power of His resurrection" (Phil. 3:10). He will direct our paths and provide favor along the way. While agreeing that potential is possibility, love-driven leaders will still seek it out of those they lead. We must always remember the words of Christ: "With men this is impossible, but with God all things are possible" (Matt. 19:26).

Love-Driven Leadership
Is Consistent

God's love is consistent. Consistency brings comfort and stability. An inconsistent God would cause our faith to quake. Jesus Christ is the same yesterday, today, and forever. God's consistency and truth cause evil to shudder.

Leaders create a loving environment when they demonstrate love consistently. It takes only one comment such as, "How could you have made such a stupid mistake?," to damage an encouraging workplace culture. Love fosters stable leadership in the face of human failure.

The acknowledgment of error should be accompanied by teaching moments. If we are to learn from our mistakes, then a teacher must take time to review the process that led to the mistake. We can always learn from an autopsy. But there should be now, therefore, no condemnation (Rom. 8:1). When Jesus confronted the woman caught in adultery, He did not sidestep her sin, but He didn't lose it or force her to wallow in her mistake. (See John 8:10–11.)

Loving leaders do not come unglued in the face of errors or the unexpected. They are predictable. Love responds to good days and bad days without an aberration in behavior. We can trust God's loving leadership because He has assured us, "I am the LORD, I do not change" (Mal. 3:6). The immutability of God assures us. He "is not a man, that He should lie, nor a son of man, that He should repent" (Num. 23:19). All His promises are yes and amen (2 Cor. 1:20). There is "no change or shadow of turning" in Him (James 1:17). He speaks peace into the storm (Mark 4:39).

What mattered yesterday will matter today. But when a strong leader is present, a sense of calm consistently permeates the hallways. The group remains composed in the face of difficulty because of the calm of one.

An organization progresses when a steady hand is at the helm. The ship doesn't dart starboard and then suddenly shift back. The compass point is fixed even in stormy seas. The leader sets sail for the next port while making the team feel at ease.

Of course leadership is flexible and responds to opportunities, but flex can be executed with calm. In the most difficult situations love-driven leaders will emit the greatest sense of quiet confidence. A fire-tested leader doesn't seek new fires but can and will respond to any fire with calm consistency.

Consistency matters. At home, work, or play a consistent leader will enjoy better outcomes. This leader has a keen sense of how things will turn out. She knows the end by training, experience, and deep-rooted faith.

As someone who seeks to be a love-driven leader, I know that I know the Holy Spirit will lead me through and to peace. My heavenly leader calms my soul. I have great confidence in the direction the Holy Spirit is leading me. I just need to remain in Him.

Consistency cannot be faked. It is revealed. A team may not even be aware of the consistency of their leader, but the team is aware of the calm. Calm is the offspring of consistency. If we follow the leading of the Holy Spirit, our destiny is very predictable.

So this then is the case for leader love. God created us to love. It is His greatest commandment. How could we ever think about leading without a consistent display of love with action? We all need more love. Our organizations need more love.

Strong leaders love well.

Love-Driven
Leader Truths to Remember

- Effective leaders love the people they lead.

- Sometimes all that is needed to demonstrate love is a kinder tone and better language when asking for a job to be completed.

- Highly effective leaders lead well in every environment, whether in the home, in the workplace, at church, or in personal relationships.

- If leaders are to create a loving environment, love must be demonstrated consistently.

- As followers of Christ we must love others because God is love, and He commanded and created us to love.

Chapter 2

THE FAITH OF A LEADER

ABRAHAM WAITED ON the son of promise for decades, and he made his mistakes along the waiting road. When Isaac was finally born, it was another testimony of the faithfulness of God, his friend. I imagine Abraham took great joy in raising his heir, telling the boy stories of how God called him out of his country and from among his people, the adventures of rescuing Lot from the hand of the enemy kings, his encounter with Melchizedek, and the covenant God made with him.

Surely Abraham loved Isaac with everything in him—and more than his own life. But there came a day when Abraham had to make a choice: follow the leader who loved him faithfully, or follow the love in his heart for Isaac. In Genesis 22 we see the Lord testing Abraham's allegiance to the greater mission, commanding him:

Take your son, your only son Isaac, whom you love, and go to the land of Moriah, and offer him there as a burnt offering on one of the mountains of which I will tell you.

—Genesis 22:2

I can't fathom the emotions that must have flooded Abraham's soul. Yet the man of God rose up early in the morning and saddled his donkey to head out on a life-changing journey with Isaac. Every moment of wood gathering and preparation must have been filled with questions about how he could tell Sarah about the loss of their son. How could she ever understand?

Abraham didn't argue with God. We see no evidence of him begging or questioning the directions. Abraham apparently did not appeal to God in any way to change His mind. To do so would have been haughty or selfish. Abraham ensured that his heart *could not be despised*, to paraphrase Psalm 51:17—which is why what happens next is hard for any parent to read:

So Abraham took the wood of the burnt offering and laid it on Isaac his son; and he took the fire in his hand and the knife. So the two of them walked on together. But Isaac spoke to Abraham his father and said, "My father!"

And he said, "Here I am, my son."

Then he said, "Here is the fire and the wood, but where is the lamb for the burnt offering?"

Abraham said, "My son, God will provide for

Himself the lamb for a burnt offering." So the two of them went together.

Then they came to the place that God had told him. So Abraham built an altar there and arranged the wood; and he bound Isaac his son and laid him on the altar, on the wood. Then Abraham stretched out his hand and took the knife to slay his son.

—GENESIS 22:6–10

Fortunately for Isaac, God stopped Abraham just in time. Genesis 22 goes on to say:

But the angel of the LORD called to him out of heaven and said, "Abraham, Abraham!"

And he said, "Here I am."

Then He said, "Do not lay your hands on the boy or do anything to him, because now I know that you fear God, seeing you have not withheld your only son from Me."

Then Abraham lifted up his eyes and looked, and behind him was a ram caught in a thicket by his horns. So Abraham went and took the ram and offered him up as a burnt offering in the place of his son. Abraham called the name of that place The LORD Will Provide, as it is said to this day, "In the mount of the LORD it will be provided."

—GENESIS 22:11–14

In the moment of this decision we clearly see a model leader. Surely Abraham wanted to please the Lord, but wouldn't Abraham also have considered that there might possibly be another path? Leaders are constantly presented with opportunities to take an easy way out. Yet Abraham trusted God enough to obey Him even when it hurt.

With every step of his journey up the mountain with Isaac, Abraham grew in faith as he trusted that God would provide an answer. Abraham didn't know the answer, but he knew God. Consider Hebrews 11:19: "He reasoned that God was able to raise him up, even from the dead, from which he indeed received him in a figurative sense."

> **Godly leaders "reason" by faith that God is in control of every decision point in their lives.**

Abraham's faith was active in his reasoning. It extended beyond any natural tendency to question and doubt. At the moment of testing Abraham did not exhibit a crisis of faith.

Many leaders are called to make decisions that test their faith. Godly leaders "reason" by faith that God is in control of every decision point in their lives. Prayer fuels the faith of a leader, and action demonstrates our obedience to God's will.

Abraham didn't have to sacrifice his son at an altar. But his willingness to do so positioned him for God's abundant blessings in his life, in Isaac's life, and in the lives of all his descendants. We read in Genesis 22:15–18:

> Then the angel of the LORD called to Abraham out of heaven a second time, and said, "By Myself I have sworn, says the LORD, because you have done this thing, and have not withheld your son, your only son, I will indeed bless you and I will indeed multiply your descendants as the stars of the heavens and as the sand that is on the seashore. Your descendants will possess the gate of their enemies. Through your offspring all the nations of the earth will be blessed, because you have obeyed My voice."

Faith in Discomfort

When leaders reach a plateau in their personal growth, the organization also will tend to flatline. Leaders must be open to hearing the voice of God directing them to "go from your country, your family, and your father's house to the land that I will show you" (Gen. 12:1). Abraham heard this message at age seventy-five.

We cannot conclude that God requires only young people to pack up the moving truck. The trip from Haran to Canaan for Abram and his wife, Sarai (their names before God changed them to Abraham and Sarah), must have been difficult. The aging couple didn't have a comfortable trip for their tired bodies, and they weren't bolstered by bottles of nutraceuticals.

But God loves to lead us out of our comfort zones. The Lord seems to draw us into places and situations in which learning will be a necessity. Leaders, take note. If we aren't struggling with opportunities, projects, or people, it's possible we have reached a plateau. How long will a team follow a leader who has dropped anchor into the safety of sameness?

One of the problems with a leader plateau is recognizing that fact. Leaders stuck on a treadmill may believe they are headed somewhere. Their legs are moving, their breathing is elevated, and it feels as if progress is being made. Unfortunately the scenery isn't changing. Everyone is doing what he has always done.

> **God loves to lead us out of our comfort zones.**

The organization has become comfortable and probably resistant to change.

God moved Abraham so he could grow for a kingdom purpose that would soon be revealed. Moving is a learning experience. And once things begin moving, progress for the organization and the kingdom begins to accelerate. Throughout the year it's important to take inventory of our terrain. Are we climbing? Have our surroundings become too familiar? Are the people around us growing? We cannot move toward our vision without moving.

Love-driven leaders must not be risk-averse. We've been instructed to "take up our cross and die daily." (See Matthew 16:24; Luke 9:23.) What has more risk than dying daily? When we fear risk, we present a selfish motive. We fear loss or embarrassment. Even if we rationalize our unwillingness to take risks for fear of how it might affect the organization, the fear of risk still seems to indicate a crisis of faith.

Let's explore this further. Why do we tend to welcome less risk as we age? Could it be that we are fearful of losing something we have stored in our moving trucks? Are we in asset-protection mode? Opportunities to serve are filled with inherent risk. We fear criticism, rebuke, and isolation. Mostly we fear exposure to the elements.

After Elijah humiliated the prophets of Baal at Mount

Carmel, he fled into the wilderness when Jezebel threatened to kill him. He went a day's journey then lay down under a juniper tree.

Elijah's juniper tree offered peace and only the risk of the bite of a bug. But just when the rest became comfortable, an angel of the Lord appeared and asked, "Why are you here, Elijah?" (1 Kings 19:13).

That's what God in His mercy does to us. Just when we get comfortable, He'll ask us, "What are you doing here? Are you afraid of that Jezebel? Has the risk moved you off mission? I thought I heard you singing just last week, 'I shall not be moved.'"

I've heard many sermons on why Elijah fled from Jezebel to hide under a tree and then in a cave. Most people tend to suggest that Elijah was afraid that Jezebel would kill him, as she'd promised. Perhaps he had only lost his zeal to lead. His experience under the tree was preceded by one of the highlights of his leadership career. Attacks often follow a big win.

Truly the riskiest moment of a leader's life is the moment that fear of risk freezes his walk. Friends caution me frequently that if I keep up my current pace, I will burn out. I tend to swat away that risk as a pesky tree bug. When I see through the eyes of my body, it is easy to identify many layers of risk in almost everything I could attempt. I took a lot of risks just driving to my office this morning. Someone could have run a red light.

When I see with the eyes of the Spirit, my vision is corrected to twenty-twenty. I see godly outcomes and know in whom I put my trust. God called me to this great opportunity. He gifted me for just this moment. I know that God is for me. Who can be against me? I walk in favor.

> **The riskiest moment of a leader's life is the moment that fear of risk freezes his walk.**

The Holy Spirit will keep you moving. Think new thoughts. Pray new prayers. Ask God to give you a fresh anointing within your calling.

Step Out and Cross Over

Abraham set out on a long journey of love. The Bible calls him a Hebrew (Gen. 14:13). The root of the Hebrew word for *Hebrew* is *Ivri*, which literally means to cross over. Abraham left his comfort zone, crossed boundaries, and set out on a voyage with Jehovah.[1]

When we make a journey of any significant distance, we will certainly notice a change in terrain. We will cross boundaries real and imagined. Love-driven leaders must be prepared to cross difficult paths. The days of "I lead; you follow" are long gone. Few leaders work in an environment of isolation. Today's leader must be a bridge-builder across multiple teams, functions, and geographies. Abraham's faith built a bridge to bless not only the Hebrews but also the Gentiles (Gal. 3:14).

Leaders must be bridge-builders as they help create good work flow and commitment among all communities. An environment that nurtures "us versus them" within an organization is toxic and harmful to the sustainability of the mission.

We must learn to lead across groups. The key is to find an intersection between independence and dependence. Expertise may be diverse, but the outcome must be common.

Networks are created by design. Is any network more important than the one among our internal teams? Some leaders miss this concept so badly that each team is given different-colored T-shirts to magnify allegiance to one department over another. Homesteading and isolationism have gone the way of dinosaurs and eight-track tapes.

We must celebrate our differences while embracing alignment. We must connect the dots without losing the beauty of each individual dot. We must produce today while empowering vision. We must share our identity while stimulating the individual. Like

Abraham, love-driven leaders adapt to new terrain. Boundaries must blur.

Leaders improvise. The ability to stand on a stage and perform improv comedy or theater is often referred to as a talent. When we watch a person onstage receive a small thread of an idea and turn it into a story or comedy routine, many think this behavior is a gift.

As leaders we tend to be focused on our plans and send our teams in a particular direction to achieve a specific target. We've written goals and set strategies. At some point during every year we are awakened to a reality of unforeseen obstacles. Things aren't going as planned. When Lot was captured by enemy kings, Abraham had to stop what he was doing and address the crisis. He didn't fret and worry. He made a plan and executed it. (See Genesis 14:13–16.)

Effective leaders have learned to make course adjustments on the fly. Leaders who adjust well tend to be more successful. Those leaders who focus on the wringing of hands and the unfairness of a thing tend to fizzle out. Quick response to market conditions or other intrusions is not an issue of talent. We aren't born with a gift to zig and zag. Experience teaches leaders that things rarely go as planned.

Good planning documents include a lifeboat scenario. We think and prepare for what could happen. But above all that we think or do, we have the Holy

Spirit to lead us in a new direction with a well-lit path. There are no surprises in the kingdom of God. If we remain diligent in our prayer and Bible study life, it's not likely that we will miss the need to make a course correction.

I believe God's favor helps us with our vision. It's the spiritually blind who are often shocked or surprised by changing climates. It should be hard to sneak up on a leader who is led by the Holy Spirit. I don't need to be talented at improv. God tells me that I can do it. Let this be your prayer: "Lord, help me remain fully dependent upon the Holy Spirit to direct my path."

Cover Your Team

God desires leaders who will seek His face. Common leadership principles are useful to accomplish temporal goals. Leading a team to accomplish spiritual goals requires a dependence on hearing the voice of God. I have heard from the Lord throughout my career. Whether it was at a television station, in a restaurant, or at a pulpit, I know that I know I was led by the Holy Spirit. The Lord said in Ezekiel 22:30, "I sought for a man among them who would build up the hedge and stand in the gap before Me for the land so that I would not destroy it, but I found no one."

Isn't it sad that God was seeking but could not find anyone to stand in the gap to protect His people? Not one man would demonstrate the faith to build a hedge around the land. Love-driven leaders are the first to stand in the gap to protect their team. Leader love takes hits without hesitation. The promise of covering is implied in the job title.

"I've got you covered" is a popular expression that rarely means anything spiritual. Its meaning may range from "I'll pay for your lunch" to "I'm praying for you." We know the blood of Jesus covered our sins once and for all. But the covering of love-driven leadership includes prayers, correction, and service in faith.

Love-driven leaders are quick to pray for the needs of the team. Leader love intercedes.

Covering includes a willingness to correct and coach. To leave a team untrained and vulnerable shows a measurable lack in leadership.

Serving others is perhaps the best form of covering. A leader with a servant's heart sees gaps and creates action to meet needs. There are many gaps in the workplace. Many hedges need to be built, including a hedge of prayer.

Faithful Leaders Are Willing to Sacrifice

When we read or hear stories of faithful sacrifice, the stories usually include some terrible loss of life on behalf of another. Somehow it seems to motivate us because one person had the courage to die for another.

Author and pastor Bryan Chapell tells this story that happened in his hometown: Two brothers were playing on the sandbanks by the river. One ran after the other up a large mound of sand. Unfortunately the mound was not solid, and their weight caused them to sink in quickly.

When the boys did not return home for dinner, the family and neighbors organized a search. They found the younger brother unconscious, with his head and shoulders sticking out above the sand. When they cleared the sand to his waist, he awakened. The searchers asked, "Where is your brother?" The child replied, "I'm standing on his shoulders." [2]

In business we don't hear many stories about one business dying in order to save the life of another existing business. Competition is known to be fierce and brutal. The depth of sacrifice in business may not be greater than doing without an expense account for a season while waiting for revenue to increase.

There aren't courses in business schools that teach sacrifice as an important tool for young leaders to quickly develop. Students may not even hear the word *sacrifice* during their training. The connotation of the application of sacrifice usually begins with a boss informing his team: "We all will need to take pay cuts in order for this business to survive. That's the only way we can save the company."

Organizational sacrifices tend to show up in finances and department head counts. As we read stories and hear about the stock options and high compensation of leaders, few of us believe the executive leadership experiences anything close to personal sacrifice. Most hard-working employees would not find it easy to believe their business leader makes any sacrifice whatsoever for the good of the company.

> **Leader love finds ways to sacrifice anything other than people who are doing the work of the organization.**

Yet love begins with giving up something of value. It may be time, money, or personal preferences that are first sacrificed for the greater good. When a leader stops to listen to the plea of a line worker, the leader is sacrificing other work to demonstrate love by listening to a team member.

When a leader makes budget cuts without affecting the income of her team, she puts people above other pressing needs in the department. Leader love finds ways to sacrifice anything other than people who are doing the work of the organization.

Leaders are called upon to "die to self" in almost

any meeting. Leader love must set aside personal preferences to allow others at the table to try things the leader doesn't really want to do. Sometimes it's more important to allow a team member to grow than it is to launch pet projects.

Abraham's demonstration of faith was accented by personal sacrifice. Faith involves more than belief. A leader who is full of faith will be noted for taking actions that require personal sacrifice. Leaders die daily for the good of the vision and mission. Loving leaders lead in faith and are willing to die to self.

Love-Driven Leader
Truths to Remember

- Leaders are often called to make decisions that test their faith.

- Leaders must be willing to sacrifice comfort for growth.

- The fear of risk could be a symptom of a faith crisis.

- As a leader you must think new thoughts, pray new prayers, and ask the Holy Spirit to give you fresh anointing in your calling.

- Loving leaders are willing to die to self for the good of their teams.

Chapter 3

RELATIONSHIPS
PRECEDE INFLUENCE

THE ESSENCE OF leadership is influence. Without influence a leader will resort to using fear and intimidation as a means to an end. The advent of Theory X in management was simply an outgrowth of an era of leaders who felt workers wouldn't do their best without the use of a carrot and stick for proper motivation.[1]

Threatening job loss was and probably still is the way many managers motivate workers. But most leaders have learned that fear accelerates turnover. Yelling and screaming at a team to "work harder" yields only temporary compliance, at best.

Influence begins in a leader's heart. I don't know if it is possible to influence anyone in the long run without demonstrating a wheelbarrow full of care and compassion. The abundance of my heart is demonstrated in the manner in which I speak and take action. It is a combination of words and actions that builds a relationship.

I cannot simply command a relationship into existence. Relationships are crafted over time, and the fruit of the relationship is influence. I think many would-be leaders miss the fact that influence is a two-way street in the same way that relationships are mutually beneficial.

> **Relationships are the seed for the fruit of influence.**

To be a person of influence, I must first be willing to be influenced by the needs of those I hope to lead. Leaders don't say: "Let me influence you. See how hard I work and how much I care? Now follow me!" Meaningful care is demonstrated more than spoken.

Relationships are the seed for the fruit of influence. Leaders must focus on the needs of work teams. There is a time and place to focus on the efficacy of the work, but the antecedent of a highly effective work team is a leader's influence on the group. A matrix of influence exists because a leader birthed a culture of meaningful relationships. The leader's care must be felt within each work station. Every member of a team must feel the flow of his leader's concern over time.

Relationships Are Built Over Time

When Jacob encountered Rachel at the well, it was love at first sight. Their first kiss was in the field among sheep, and he was soon invited back home to meet her dad. Laban offered Jacob a job, saying, "Tell me, what shall your wages be?" (Gen. 29:15). Jacob wasn't interested in riches. Love inspired him to win Rachel's heart.

> Jacob loved Rachel, so he said, "I will serve you seven years for Rachel your younger daughter." Laban said, "It is better that I give her to you than that I should give her to another man. Stay with me." So Jacob served seven years for Rachel, and they seemed to him but a few days because of the love he had for her.
>
> —Genesis 29:18–20

Unbeknownst to Jacob, whose name means "supplanter"—one who supersedes another, especially by force or treachery[2]—he was about to be supplanted himself. Perhaps Jacob was reaping the seed he sowed when he stole the birthright from his twin brother, Esau. Or perhaps he was learning how leader love doesn't operate.

After the seven years were fulfilled, Jacob asked Laban for Rachel. Laban tricked him by taking his other daughter, Leah, into Jacob's tent. When Jacob woke up the next morning and found Leah instead of Rachel, he was disappointed but was still determined to marry Rachel. The price: seven more years of service to Laban.

God loved us by preparing the way. He devised a plan to reconcile mankind to Himself even before He began a relationship with us. Jacob's situation, however unpleasant, also prepared him to lead. Jacob demonstrated a love that was willing to prepare and wait for God's perfect timing.

Jacob decided in his heart that Rachel was to be his priority. We demonstrate our priorities by the way we choose to invest our time. I've often said that if you show me your day planner, I will tell you what is important to you. Jacob showed his love by the way he set his time priorities. He blocked off another seven years to ensure Rachel was in his life.

Sometimes we set mutually exclusive goals. Time is a depleting resource, and the time we invest to reach one goal will deplete the time we have available to reach a second or third goal. A leader must consider how his team makes time decisions. Is the team working on the right project at the right time? But more importantly, are you prioritizing your time to build a strong relationship with your team? Leaders are leaders in time allocation.

Relationships Are Baked in the Trenches

I spent much of my career serving as a college professor. I suppose it could be said that a professor is a leader of students, but that would suggest there is a following. College students are reluctant followers of anyone.

I taught my first college class at around age twenty-four. I was finishing work on my master of business administration and was given the opportunity to teach the History of American Economics. This was horrific on several different levels. It was a freshman-level course, with football players huddling in the back row. I was 130 pounds of nervousness, insecurity, and incompetence. Perhaps my skinny knees knocked a few times on that first day.

The course was part history and part economics. Neither topic seemed riveting to my students, who only a few months prior had been celebrating high school graduation. The textbook was about twenty pounds of words with only a few pictures. So this was also a reading class.

After that first, nightmare of a class I went to see my department head. He was three times my age and balding, and he led with love. He always spoke through a knowing smile. He called me "young lad" as long as I knew him. If only he could see my geezer appearance now.

I told him I didn't know how to teach. How could I teach a college class without ever taking a course on teaching? He told me something I've shared with managers, leaders, and young faculty in the years since then. He said: "Young lad, you've just got to remember the good teachers you had and do what they did. Then think about the teachers you didn't like so well, and don't do what they did. Remember, your textbook is a guide to open young minds to learning. Be a learning leader." Then he handed the book back to me and said, "Go teach your class."

When I walked into my next class in Tinsley Hall, room 203, I felt my heart pounding in my chest, and I knew with certainty that I was called to be a teacher. I knew in that moment I would spend my life teaching. In time I would earn a doctoral degree and become a leader of learning.

In 2008 I was called to Oral Roberts University (ORU) to serve as the dean of the College of Business and of online learning. I had been teaching as an adjunct instructor for a couple of years, but in 2008 events took place at the college that led to a vacancy in the leadership. Dr. Mark Rutland had just been appointed president of the university, and I was the first person he hired.

As a dean I was fortunate to also be needed in the classroom. I taught several classes in our undergraduate marketing program as well as in the master of business administration program. I had been away from the classroom for many years prior to teaching at ORU. While working in the marketplace, I had the

opportunity to work with many young college gradu-
ates. I've hired people in twenty-seven markets. I've seen
them come and go. So I think I developed an understanding of why young recruits were not doing well in
their first jobs. Most young college grads catch the enti-
tlement virus. Perhaps they feel that they've paid their
dues and the time has come to collect the spoils.

> **I was able to influence my students
> not simply because I was their
> professor but because I had built
> relationships with them.**

I tried to teach my students about the difficulties
and further preparation needed to develop as a human
resource asset. I taught life skills necessary to succeed
in business. We talked about simple things such as
writing personal thank-you notes, getting to work early,
doing more than asked, and building relationships at
every opportunity.

I was able to influence my students not simply
because I was their professor but because I had built
relationships with them. I took a personal interest in
their lives. I chose to be accessible outside the classroom. I was hard-nosed about meetings in my office
and required students to set appointments, and then
I kept those meetings relatively formal. I wanted to

replicate a business office more than a faculty office. But out of the classroom and the office I chose to get to know my students and allow them to get to know me.

I visited with students in the deli almost daily at breakfast and/or lunch. My wife and I enjoyed dinner with students at least once a week in their cafeteria. I would send out a tweet before heading to the cafeteria and ask my students to find me if they wanted to chat. My wife and I sat at different tables each time and got to know future leaders from all over the world.

I visited male students in the lobbies of their dorms. We prayed and sang worship songs, but we mostly cut up. I still laugh as I think about what I learned about dorm life during those times. (It wasn't anything like dorm life in the early seventies!)

I went to intramural football, basketball, and volley-ball games in which my students were playing. I didn't say or do much. I just wanted them to see me in the stands. I like sports, so it wasn't a sacrifice for me to support their games.

My wife and I regularly invited students into our home. She's a great cook, and no matter what she prepared, there were never leftovers. At various seasons we had a student living in our upstairs rooms. It was a private and safe environment for them.

I've also had the honor of presiding over many of my students' weddings. In most cases I taught both the bride and the groom and oversaw their premarital counseling. My wife and I continue our relationship with many of those couples. I have pictures of first dogs to prove this claim.

Sadly I was needed to preside over funerals of too many students I had grown to love and lead. We lost three young men and a faculty member in a plane crash in Chanute, Kansas, on a Friday afternoon in May 2012. The students were on their way to minister at a Teen Mania conference and were killed less than a week after their graduation. I still do not understand much about this tragedy. I continue to mourn the loss of these and other young leaders.

I also mourn the loss of ORU alum Jordan Lewis to cancer. He was the son of dear friends Ron and Lynette Lewis, the latter of whom served on ORU's board of trustees. There is much to tell about Jordan, but in this book I will speak only of the fact that in his short life he led with love. His fellow students, colleagues, wife, family, and church friends all knew him as a gentle, caring man with a mighty influence. His influence multiplied as he welcomed new relationships and saw the best in every person he met. I am thankful to have known this leader of men. His memory influences me every day.

In fact, the memory of every student I have met along my journey remains with me. Thankfully I only remember the good days, moments, and lessons learned in and outside of the classroom. I can say with great confidence that my students taught me how to lead with love. I honor them with this book.

Over time I have learned that although I was a marketing professor, I was teaching the value of personal relationships in every career stop. I have contact about every month with people from my first class on through my tenure at ORU. I don't think of my students as friends, though we are. But it's deeper than that. We baked our relationships in an oven of high expectations and servant leadership.

Leaders' relationships are built on the trust earned in the trenches. In the middle of their hardest days of teaching, learning, and doing they built trust with others. And isn't that the essence of a work team? Trust is more than a concept. Servant-leaders build trusting relationships through actions.

Setting the Right Priorities

Loving leadership requires setting priorities. Jacob had his priorities in order. His love for Rachel constrained Him. Likewise the love of the Lord should constrain us to redeem the time "because the days are evil" (Eph. 5:16). That means setting the right priorities. Jacob didn't let anything get in the way of his heart's desire to win Rachel.

We show love by our nos as well as our yeses. Leaders who love are intentional about carving out time to develop deep relationships with teammates. It is never a waste of time to make time to listen to teammates. If Jacob had shifted his priorities at any time and given up his plan, what would have happened to Israel? God gives us the time to do His will. He expects us to demonstrate good stewardship with our choices on how to use the time we've been given.

Ask almost any leader what he wants most at the office, and the answer will be some version of, "I just want more time to do the things I need to do." However, more time may not be the answer to getting more done.

My observation is that the greatest enemy of effective time management is the continual flow of interruptions or distractions. Distractions usually come in the form of technology. I frequently teach about the ever-present threat of the tech "doom loop." We stop to check e-mail, Facebook, Twitter, text messages, and various apps. By the time we finish checking everything, it's time to check e-mail again, and therein lies the loop.

Interruptions from outside the office door often only interrupt the distractions disguised as progress (such as the tech doom loop). Leaders can protect themselves from interruptions better than from distractions. Some of us have a guard at the gate. Some leaders require appointments. Other leaders have an always-open door to encourage interruption of the distractions.

Like most leaders I've resigned myself to thinking I'm not going to be able to make proactive progress between the hours of eight and five. It seems the big stuff happens early, late, and on weekends. But I have made one addition to my work plan for the day that may be useful for you.

I set aside one hour of each day that I call my "zero hour." During the hour I have zero tolerance for distractions. No tech, no e-mail, no nothing but proactive thinking, writing, or doing. I prefer to have no interruptions during zero hour, but I'm not always able to control my door. Remember, a zero hour happens during work hours when the office is full.

During this time I'm holding myself accountable to get away from my computer screens and phone and shut down for an hour of progress. I do not allow myself any excuses for breaking my rules during zero hour. I've been amazed at how one simple hour can make such an impact on progress.

But I also want to mention the most important hour of the day, which occurs before anyone is in the office with me. Most of you have a similar time. Mine is called a "power hour." It is during this hour that I spend time building the most important relationship of all. During this hour I have my devotions and prayer time. I intercede for those I have committed to praying for, and the list is long. I also pray for every member of my team by name every morning.

When I watched the movie *War Room*, I was encouraged to enhance my prayer time by writing scriptures to read as I make specific requests and claims for others. I find I spend very little time on "bless me, bless me," need-based prayers. I can pray those prayers all day. The power hour is devoted to others. I depend upon my power hour to launch my day and receive the spiritual assignments God has for me. I have no distractions and no interruptions. Perhaps a zero hour and a power hour could be useful in your day.

Distractions delay the execution of a plan. Think of Samuel as he was preparing to anoint Saul to become king. Donkeys belonging to Saul's father, Kish, had escaped and were lost. Considering the times, I suppose the loss was roughly equivalent to losing a car or two from the driveway. I think that would qualify as a distraction.

I can imagine the conversation a worker would have if he encountered a problem such as the one Kish faced: "I know we planned to meet today to consider our growth plans for the second quarter, but both of our cars were stolen from our driveway. There's no way I can meet today."

There is a common collision between our plans

for the day and the spiritual appointments set for us. We often confuse the important with the urgent. The people who surround a leader will rarely understand a decision to move in a spiritual assignment instead of responding to the myriad of highly urgent demands in the workplace.

Saul had been looking all over for his father's donkeys. For three days he and his father's servants had been searching high and low. When they came to the land of Zuph, they remembered that the prophet lived there, so they decided to ask him where the donkeys could be found.

Long before Saul knocked on Samuel's door, God had told the prophet He was sending a man to him who was to be anointed king of Israel. When Saul arrived, his mind was still on the donkeys, but the Lord had brought him to Samuel for something much more important. The prophet Samuel actually had to tell Saul to stop worrying about the lost donkeys so he could get him to focus on the more significant matter at hand (1 Sam. 9:20).

God had a higher purpose for Saul's wild donkey chase, one that he might have missed had he been unwilling to redirect his focus from his father's agenda to God's plans for him. As leaders we must take up a sword against the agendas of others. We must find the most important spiritual task of the day and dedicate our full energy to affect its completion.

> **Godly time management
> is spiritual warfare.**

It's not hard to discern the spiritual agenda of the day. It is assigned through prayer and daily Bible reading. A spiritual assignment rarely comes by e-mail, text, or voice mail. It comes directly into our hearts and likely consumes us.

The more I focus on completing spiritual assignments, the more God is faithful to redeem the time and somehow make the path easier to complete marketplace assignments. Spending the day chasing donkeys is the path of least resistance. But moving toward a spiritual priority requires resisting the temptation to respond to the urgent. Godly time management is spiritual warfare.

Our time is well spent when we cultivate relationships that lead to influence. When we stop being too busy to care more, our relationships and influence will enjoy marked improvement.

Learning to Say No

Jacob served many others before he was released to lead his home and his nation. His spiritual training was connected to the manual labor he performed for Laban. Jacob's relationship with his father-in-law became complicated because of Laban's dishonesty and greed. Jacob told his wives, "Your father has deceived me and changed my wages ten times" (Gen. 31:7).

Most leaders have to learn similar lessons along the way when it comes to working with people. Jacob's story had soap-operatic twists and turns, but after twenty long years of service Jacob was prepared to lead—and part of that preparation was learning to say no. When the Lord told Jacob, "Return to the land of your fathers, to your family, and I will be with you" (Gen. 31:3), Jacob did not consult with the cheating Laban. With God's help Jacob finally learned to say no.

I believe Jacob learned to say no to temptations that would alter his time priorities. Three questions could determine your productivity today: (1) Can you fit me in?, (2) Can you fit in another meeting?, and (3) Can you fit this into your to-do list today? There's a lot of *fitting in* happening in organizations today, and that's not a good thing. Somehow we've come to think, "If I *can* fit it in, I *should* fit it in." Life seems cluttered with "shoulds."

Highly effective leaders say no with much more resolve than average leaders do—but love leaders say it in a way that improves relationships. We learn much about a leader's growth potential based on what he

won't do. Effective leaders make room to make a difference. They don't fill up a to-do list with more than one
thing that must be done today.

I make a list of everything that must be done
someday. But I will choose what day to do a thing
based upon priorities. Obviously I get much more than
one thing done every day. Daily routine takes care of
many things some leaders would place on a list. I have
a calendar and a good feel for what needs to happen on
what days. And I have my all-important *one thing*.

Intentionally completing one thing every day is much
better than rewriting a full to-do list tomorrow. The
good thing about a *someday* list is that I can choose to
complete that list on the right days. I'm not obligating
myself to fit in everything today. I have an ironclad
contract to complete one thing. All the rest will wait.

> **The courage to say no opens the door to
> say yes to the things God will send to us.**

I miss terrific opportunities, I'm sure. I will miss
a few meetings that occur, and the meetings will be
fine without me. I miss a few texts, phone calls, and
Facebook messages. By saying no more often, I open up
more time margin for divine appointments, relationship building, and unexpected crises. I have more time

to do important things and try not to be consumed with the urgent.

We have the right and obligation to say no. The courage to say no opens the door to say yes to the things God will send to us. Jesus told us to come out from among them—to be separate. Jesus doesn't ask us to fit in or to fit everything into a demanding schedule.

Relationships develop with intentional allocation of time resources. It's difficult to influence someone I don't spend time with. The time we spend to develop a relationship is time well spent. Influence is the fruit that blossoms from sowing seeds of time.

Love-Driven Leader
Truths to Remember

- Influence begins with a relationship. Relationships are the seeds for the fruit of influence.

- We demonstrate our priorities by the way we choose to invest our time.

- Leaders' relationships are built on the trust earned in the trenches. In the middle of their hardest days of teaching, learning, and doing they built trust with others.

- We show love by our nos as well as our yeses.

- Godly time management is spiritual warfare.

Chapter 4

MANAGING ENTROPY

Whatever we love, we want to sustain. All love begins with the hope that "this will never end." In the early days of a relationship we work to win the return of love. I wrote my best love letters to my wife before we were married. I declared my love to her in every way I could imagine. I was the love leader in the beginning of the relationship.

I recall courting a few jobs throughout my career as well. I didn't write poems and such, but I wrote marketing plans and shared strategic thinking. When I was hired, I never wanted the relationship to end. Employer and employee were a match made in heaven.

I feel that way about everyone on my team (well, most of the time). I don't want them to leave. I care about them and invest time in them to help them grow. I value my work relationships and nurture them. Love is a sustaining agent.

Yet people leave. Many people live with a "walk-about" approach. We could call them wanderers. They wander, attach to something for a while, then move on to something else. Perhaps wandering is their coping mechanism.

Organizations also wander without the steady hand of a love-driven leader. Organizations, households, and just about any relationship move toward decline every day. Science has a name for this malaise of organisms. It's called entropy, "a process of degradation or running down or a trend to disorder."[1] The entropic process explains why love can end if it is not given proper attention.

Entropy is what all organizations and organisms must fight against. The second law of thermodynamics loosely holds that all matter moves toward disorganization. Organizations tend to become disorganized.

> **Entropy: "a process of degradation or running down or a trend to disorder."**

Consider a closet in a home. It is cleaned on a spring holiday. The result is a nice, neat space for everything, and everything is in place. How long does it take for the closet to become disorganized? The answer to that question is largely an issue of concern to the closet organizer.

The job of the closet leader is to create negative entropy. That is also the job of leaders. Love abounds

51

and growth continues only when the leader is intentional about growth. It is a matter of endurance. We must endure through success and the inevitable storms that fuel decay and dissolution. A love-driven leader grabs a lifeline and works with great attention to sustain the heartbeat of the organization.

Negative entropy can occur only when we take action. Sometimes the action is something internal for the leader. Circumstances may impact an organization, and the leader feels an inherent need for a change. Often the impact of entropy creates a need to redesign systems and processes.

Vibrant, healthy organizations with a loving leader at the helm can achieve negative entropy. Loving actions are intentional. Negative entropy is only achieved by diligent intention.

Moses experienced the effect of entropy. But when he did, he submitted himself to be stretched for service in ways he didn't think he could. He was a reluctant but powerful leader. He was a love-driven leader who fought for Israel's survival even as the nation seemed focused on self-destruction—or catalyzing its entropic destiny.

Ultimately Moses persevered because he saw Him who is invisible. Moses's faith and his strong desire to sustain his people kept him focused on God. God was Moses's source to lead his people toward negative entropy.

One of the fruits of faith is endurance. Leaders who love have a basic instinct to keep pressing forward even in the face of distractions and storms. Love is a powerful motivating force to charge forward. Moses loved his people so much that he led them through the wilderness without personally experiencing the Promised Land. He led them to a place he had never been to and would never reach. Great humility and wisdom were key markers of Moses's character.

Moses displayed a habit of making the right choice. We all make choices every day. The first choice is to decide whether to be led by the flesh or the spirit. We choose to set our minds and conversations on things pertaining to the flesh or to focus our attention upon the leading of the Holy Spirit. We don't accidentally follow the desires of the flesh. We make decisions to allow our sinful nature the opportunity to govern. It is impossible to serve two masters. We decide to be on the side that satisfies God or the side that satisfies our flesh. This is an important point of differentiation for leaders. We need to be clear about what team we support. We can't begin the day on one team and then change uniforms at halftime. We cannot wear the pants of one team and the jersey of another. We must declare our allegiance. One team hurries entropy, while the other works hard to slow the process of decay.

Moses was a leader who abided in the kingdom of God, and he was deliberate about pursuing things that are invisible and eternal. His mind was set upon things above. Leaders such as Moses will declare openly, "There is nothing on earth that I desire besides You" (Ps. 73:25). This primary goal is the essence of sustainability. When desires float away from godliness, decay is sure to accelerate.

The leader who is Holy Spirit–led will have a different priority list. He will be deliberate in pursuit of things spiritual. He will surround himself with people who are moving toward godly purposes and dare not be distracted by earthly pursuits. The habits of a spiritual leader are predictable and consistent. The spiritually motivated leader will not be moved.

A pastor once told me the hardest thing he faces every day is remaining in the kingdom of God. It is not about eating and drinking. The flesh has power to consume. A love-driven leader will seek righteousness, peace, and joy as his primary sustenance and motivation (Rom. 14:17).

Godly leaders begin with a mind-set to press on toward righteousness. Our primary metrics will be peace and joy. We will ask ourselves, "Is this the right thing to do? Does this decision foster peace? Will we walk in joy as we go?" Take a page from Moses's playbook, and remain in the kingdom as you lead. The kingdom of God will not experience entropy.

Moaners, Groaners, and Naysayers Accelerate Entropy

Moses experienced what many leaders experience: moaners, groaners, gripers, and complainers. Although more opposition is found in a valley, desert, or wilderness, some employees will find something to complain about even on the mountaintop of victory.

The Israelites were vocal grumblers. They complained about Moses's vision for entering the Promised Land after Pharaoh upped their quota and deadlines (Exod. 5:1–22). They complained as the Egyptian army pursued them (Exod. 14:11–12). They complained about bitter water (Exod. 15:22). They complained about being hungry (Exod. 16:1–4). They complained about being thirsty (Exod. 17:1–4) and more.

> **Our work teams must be led out of the comfort of expected results.**

The Israelites lobbed false accusations at Moses (Num. 16:41). Even Moses's own brother and sister turned against his leadership (Num. 12:1–12). And when it was time to enter the Promised Land, ten of the twelve spies brought back an evil, unbelieving report (Num. 13:32). Moaners, groaners, and naysayers surround every step of progress. As we attempt to climb a mountain, we will surely experience the clawing hands of ankle grabbers who want to pull us down.

Moses was charged with moving people out of the status quo—out of the bondage of old ideas that had stopped working—and into the Promised Land. He was mocked for trying to fight entropy. The Israelites fought him almost every step of the way. They were always ready to run back to what they knew for fear of what they didn't know. The status quo is comfortable, predictable, and limiting. Our work teams must be led out of the comfort of expected results. A team begins to move backward the moment the cloud of comfort settles in. That's one reason it took the Israelites forty years to make a forty-day journey and a generation died without seeing the promise.

Moses in the Marketplace?

We see these same behaviors in the marketplace today. I've worked with more than eighty broadcast television stations as a consultant or an employee. The proof of performance for most television marketers is, "We're number one!" The Nielsen ratings provide support for boasts of having the largest viewing audience, allowing networks to claim, "More people watch our news than any other television station in town" and "We are your number one news source."

I enjoyed competing with the top station in a market. Number one stations don't realize when entropy has set in. Overall I found market leaders to be complacent and quite aware of their market dominance. They believed their own press clippings. Undoubtedly their teams burned jet fuel on their way to the top. My strategy for growth when competing with a number one station was to chew away at an Achilles' heel of market dominance. Marketers of a number one station begin to run out of ideas. Some marketers don't work hard enough at what matters most while they enjoy a tailwind of success.

Television program advertisers will move allegiance for one better idea, and it doesn't take long to create one powerful new idea. Ideas move money from station to station. Nothing is as powerful as a new, big idea. Ideas create negative entropy.

"Roman candle leadership" is focused on the glare of bright explosions in the sky. Everything is great until the fuel experiences entropy. Gravity eventually takes over, and what's left of the rocket falls onto the ground as tattered paper. It takes a leader to sustain the burn. Becoming a market-leading firm is one thing; remaining in the lead requires sustained, consistent effort. The love leader has an inner feeling when things begin to decay and makes positive changes to systems.

> **Nothing is as powerful as a new, big idea. Ideas create negative entropy.**

A market-leading firm is vulnerable. What goes up must come down. Whatever helped it arrive at a winning position is very difficult to sustain. It seems inevitable that the team will stop doing the things that led to success. How difficult is it for sports teams to win on a consistent basis?

Love-filled leaders must take a lesson from Moses and create new energy and negative entropy to lead their teams into growth instead of decline.

Love-Driven Leader
Truths to Remember

- Organizations, households, and just about any relationship move toward decline.

- Moses chose to remain in the kingdom as he led. The kingdom of God will not experience entropy.

- Negative entropy is achieved with sustained, consistent effort.

- Nothing is as powerful as a new, big idea. Ideas create negative entropy.

- The love leader has an inner feeling when things begin to decay and makes positive changes to systems.

Chapter 5

LOVING THROUGH A CRISIS

"Moses My servant is dead" (Josh. 1:2). Joshua knew that his mentor—the meekest man on earth, a man who delivered his people out of bondage and spoke to God face-to-face, a man whom Joshua loved and who demonstrated God's love to him—was gone. But the God of Moses was calling young Joshua to rise up and lead the Israelites in a time of crisis. Jehovah was calling Joshua to lead a new generation to a place of promise through a river of doubt.

God gave Joshua a mighty promise to sustain his faith during this time of national turmoil:

> Moses My servant is dead, so now get up and cross over the Jordan—you and all this people— to the land that I am giving to the children of Israel. I have given you every place that the sole of your foot shall tread, as I said to Moses. From the wilderness and this Lebanon, as far as the great river, the River Euphrates, all the land

of the Hittites, and to the Mediterranean Sea toward the setting of the sun will be your territory. No man will be able to stand against you all the days of your life. As I was with Moses, I will be with you. I will not abandon you. I will not leave you.

—Joshua 1:2–5

What was Joshua's response? He did not draw back in fear, knowing there were giants in the Promised Land. He did not take three months to seek God for further clarity. He did not panic. During this pivotal time Joshua took command and gained fast loyalty from the ones who had just weeks earlier followed Moses:

Then Joshua commanded the officers of the people, "Pass through the midst of the camp and command the people, 'Prepare food, for in three days you will cross the Jordan to go to take possession of the land that the Lord your God is giving you to possess.'"

To the Reubenites, the Gadites, and to the half-tribe of Manasseh, Joshua said, "Remember the word that Moses the servant of the Lord commanded you: 'The Lord your God has given you a place for rest and will give this land.' Your wives, your children, and your livestock may live in the land that Moses gave you on the east side of the Jordan. But you must cross over with your brothers fully armed, your mighty men of valor, and help them, until the LORD has given your brothers rest, as He has given you, and they also have possessed the land that the LORD your God is giving to them. Then you may return to your own land and possess what Moses the servant of the LORD gave you on the east side of the Jordan where the sun rises."

They answered Joshua, "All that you command us we will do, and wherever you send us we will go. Just as we obeyed Moses in all things, we will obey you. May the LORD your God be with you, as He was with Moses! Whoever rebels against your command and disobeys your words, in all that you command him, shall be put to death. Only be strong and courageous."

—JOSHUA 1:10–18

How Love Leads in the Face of Crisis

There must be an observable difference between a leader who is worldly and a leader who knows Jesus, a leader who loves. How does a Christian leader show that he is not of this world? How does the Christian leader glorify God? Answers to these questions are not a matter of leadership style. It's all about the daily relationship between the leader and God.

This seems almost simplistic, but we can never be reminded enough that a relationship with Jesus is the most important qualification of a leader. The worldly leader leads and manages from a worldly perspective. The foundation of this leader is sinking sand. The world informs, persuades, instructs, and ultimately destroys a powerless leader. Joshua received his leadership training directly from God, who told him:

> Be strong and very courageous, in order to act carefully in accordance with all the law that My servant Moses commanded you. Do not turn aside from it to the right or the left, so that you may succeed wherever you go. This Book of the Law must not depart from your mouth. Meditate on it day and night so that you may act carefully according to all that is written in it. For then you will make your way successful, and you will be wise.
>
> —Joshua 1:7–8

A relationship with Jesus is the most important qualification of a leader.

Loving leaders have the same instructions. Our walk does not include turns to the left or right. We will succeed wherever we go as we depend upon the Lord for direction. We are also reminded to speak the Word. We are to meditate upon it day and night. We are to "act carefully according to all that is written in it."

Is there any better advice a leader could receive? When we consider that God has placed us in leadership so we might influence others, our greatest need must be to stay close to Him. Let this be your prayer: "Dear Lord, help me be a godly influence on others as You influence me."

Leaders are not allowed to panic. The broken spirit of a leader is demonstrated by his powerful response in moments of crises. Love-driven leaders need and want to be at their best when the team is at its worst. Fires are never a surprise to experienced leaders. We expect the unexpected because we have seen so many similar situations.

I respect the calm of an airline pilot as the plane enters into air turbulence: "Ladies and gentlemen, we are entering some bumpy airspace, and it's important to fasten your seat belt and remain seated. We experience this every day, and I want you to know this is normal and we have everything under control."

What if the pilot made the announcement in this manner: "Everyone get in your seat and stay there!

We've encountered windy airspace, and I'm not sure this old plane will hold together. I've never seen anything like this! I'll do my best to get us through this, but you need to know this is bad! I suggest we all pray."

Doesn't it seem true that the volume of a voice increases with the degree of leader worry? Love-motivated leaders are calm and calming in any storm because they have been trained by experiencing similar storms. In the moment of crisis a true leader gives no thought to his personal outcome. Leaders sacrifice the luxury of personal worry to quickly enact solutions for the team.

Calm, solution-oriented leadership is what Jesus modeled.

> As they sailed, He fell asleep. Then a wind storm came down on the lake, and they were filling with water, and were in danger. They came to Him and awoke Him, saying, "Master, Master, we are perishing!" Then He arose and rebuked the wind and the raging of the water. And they ceased, and there was a calm. He said to them, "Where is your faith?" Being afraid, they marveled, saying to each other, "Who then is this Man? He commands even the winds and water, and they obey Him."
>
> —LUKE 8:23–25

Honing Your Crisis
Communication Skills

If we listen closely to a leader, we should hear words that deliver focus points. There should be little doubt about what matters most. I hope leaders would speak from one page and then do everything possible to gather the team around the same page. It's important to convene at regular "focus meetings."

I cannot overstate the importance of repetition of key messages. Does anyone tire of hearing the words "I love you"? Once is not enough for any relationship to endure. Frequency matters. Verbal assurances of love and security are comforting and foundational.

We must find a way to deliver a critical message at least seven times in seven different ways. Team members learn at different paces and in different ways. The fastest way out of organizational crises is with high-level communication. In other words, meet often and talk a lot. It works at home, and it will work at work.

But consider this golden key to meeting conversations. Love-inspired leaders will be heard talking about ideas, while other leaders talk about people. Weak leaders spend time playing the blame game. Effective leaders chart a course with new ideas. The Holy Spirit will provide inspiration to move forward. When we slip into talking about people, we will surely lose spiritual unction for progress. The way forward is paved with new ideas.

Effective leaders can't be afraid to make decisions in the heat of battle. We don't demonstrate love by outward demonstrations of worry. But understand that decision making is also impacted by our view of time. The leader must always make decisions in consideration of short-term versus long-term need and impact. It's a combination of knowing what to do and knowing when to do it. Love underpins all timing issues by making others feel comfortable that "everything is under control." A love-driven leader *needs* to know his team is coping well in the midst of the storm.

> **Love-inspired leaders will be heard talking about ideas, while other leaders talk about people.**

Crisis conditions, such as the one Joshua faced when leading the Israelites into the Promised Land, require immediate response. Time is scarce in a crisis. Decisions must be made in the moment, and there is little time for research or meetings. Course adjustments must be made on the fly. When a leader is entangled in a crisis mode, the speed of action can matter more than the quality of the decision.

When a leader is considering a decision to impact

her organization over the long term, the need for speed is replaced by a need for thoughtful consideration. Time expands to allow for meetings. Alternative paths can be considered. Contingency planning is welcomed. Long-term decision making can have long-term impact. Therefore the decision requires additional thought.

Leaders fall into deeper problems when they fail to consider the impact of timing. Long-term decisions should not be made in a hurry, while a decision required for short-term impact should not be delayed.

Begin your crisis resolution meetings with this question: What is the time frame of impact for the decision we will make today? The first consideration of crisis leadership is time. Consider the words of Solomon: "To everything there is a season, a time for every purpose under heaven....He has made everything beautiful in its appropriate time" (Eccles. 3:1, 11).

Rejecting "Overwhelm"

It isn't difficult to become overwhelmed in the midst of chaos and crisis. Imagine the crowd of five thousand men who gathered to hear Jesus speak. The disciple Andrew told Jesus, "Here is a boy with five small barley loaves and two small fish, but how far will they go among so many?" (See John 6:9.)

Jesus was frequently underwhelmed by the faith His disciples showed. The disciples were frequently overwhelmed by the vision of the Lord, particularly in the sea. I suppose there is not a neutral state to being whelmed. The word means to be engulfed or submerged—as in overwhelmed. *Whelmed* is an archaic term and serves little purpose in our vocabulary because it means to be overwhelmed.

Yet the truth is that becoming overwhelmed doesn't change much about the situation. The crowd must be fed. Work must be completed. There are feet to wash. Perhaps becoming overwhelmed is selfish. It seems that Jesus wanted His disciples to be focused on the needs of others—to love others. We never seem to have enough, yet God always provides.

My friend Rebecca, who has been our office manager at Charisma Media for more than twenty-five years, created a great object lesson for the overwhelmed. She wore arm floaties to work one day. Folklore has it that she wore the floaties all day. In her brilliant teaching manner she made it clear that flotation devices are available for the overwhelmed. Sometimes effective leaders will bring laughter into chaos. I think that's the lesson here. And I believe that a loving leader finds ways to help her team manage the madness.

The Holy Spirit keeps us afloat. Jesus is our Prince of Peace. The Lord is our shepherd; we shall not want. When the job is too big, budgets are too large, and people are too whelmed, do what the disciples did. Do all that you can do, and trust the Lord to help you help your team.

A Crisis of Sin

I have a great friend. I know this to be true because he is quick to tell me things no one else would tell me. If I have spinach in my teeth, even for a moment, he will tell me. I hate looking in the mirror and seeing a leafy vegetable waving back at me.

But the pain of seeing the tree in my teeth pales in comparison to my thoughts of all the people I may have encountered since lunch, those who didn't care enough to share the obvious truth. Leaders must be willing to love by confrontation.

Weak leaders put off speaking the truth and allow an issue to develop barnacles. Quick confrontation about an error in performance is life-giving. Hearing a leader say, "You've been doing this wrong for the last month," is debilitating and trust-busting.

Corrective and loving confrontation builds trust. Jesus confronted the woman at the well after she declared she had no husband. He said, "You have had five husbands, and he whom you now have is not your husband" (John 4:18).

I wonder how many leaders today, armed with such knowledge, would be as loving in confrontation. Do you believe the woman's life was changed by this encounter? No one likes to be confronted. But we all need someone in our lives who cares enough to challenge us, especially in times of crisis.

There are times when failure in business is because of "sin in the camp" (read: poor attention to detail, a violation of policies and procedures, a lack of pursuing excellence, or some other downfall). When the Israelites suffered a crushing defeat at the hands of Ai after a series of clear victories, Joshua ripped his clothes and fell on his face in front of the ark of the Lord (Josh. 7:6). Then he confronted God:

> O Lord God, why did You bring this people across the Jordan to give us into the hands of the Amorites to destroy us? If only we had been content to dwell on the other side of the Jordan! O my Lord, what should I say now that Israel has fled before its enemies? The Canaanites and all the inhabitants of the land may hear, turn on us, and cut off our name from the earth. What will You do for Your great name?
>
> —Joshua 7:7–9

God answered, telling Joshua that Israel had sinned. One of the Israelites took things dedicated for destruction. So God instructed Joshua to confront the sin in the camp quickly—the next morning, in fact. Joshua brought each tribe forward until the culprit, Achan, was rooted out. Joshua dealt with the sin in the camp quickly, and Israel went on to win its next battle.

Four Ways to Enhance Crisis Authority

Moses was the only righteous leader the Israelites had ever known. Before Moses there was Pharaoh, a cruel taskmaster. So when Moses died, the people grieved. Could they respect Joshua's authority? Any new leader coming into an organization must earn the respect of his team.

How can you help your team learn to respect your authority in an age when respect for authority is withering away? How can you win loyalty in a time when many in authority are questioned, ignored, and even mocked? In the midst of a crisis the questioning of authority increases: "We didn't have these kinds of problems before so-and-so took over."

We can recall that the leadership of Jesus was questioned as well. "They came again to Jerusalem, and as He was walking in the temple, the chief priests and the scribes and the elders came to Him, and said, 'By what authority are You doing these things, and who gave You this authority to do them?'" (Mark 11:27–28).

This reminds me of hearing a five-year-old wailing at a store clerk who took away a toy from the little darling, "You can't take that from me! You aren't the boss of me. Give it back!" Even the "boss of him" struggled to recover the toy.

Leaders walk a slippery slope in making claim to the ownership of authority. While organization charts can define how authority *should* flow, we have all observed how informal influences within an organization can whittle away at formal authority.

The goal of a strong leader is to align the informal and formal flow of authority. Keeping an organization in alignment with the proper authority is likely one of the strongest tests of leadership. Here are four ways to help with authority alignment:

1. Make fewer statements, and ask more questions. Jesus answered the questions about His authority by asking questions (Mark 11:29–33).

2. Be inclusive. When we treat our team members like mushrooms and keep them in the dark, the light may never reach them. People in the dark tend to reject authority. Light leads to understanding and compliance.

3. Overcommunicate. Write it. Speak it. Repeat it. Draw on the walls if necessary.

4. Celebrate team wins. When teams win, leadership tends to have an easier time with submission to authority. Sports teams love their coaches as long as the teams are winning. Authority dwindles in losses.

Effective leaders help people love authority.

I think I've seen every episode of *The Andy Griffith Show*. Sometimes I miss Mayberry. Andy's show was wholesome and packed with life lessons. I also believe we could isolate many of the 249 episodes and use the footage in leadership training classes. We watch as Andy leads men and his town through life. He was probably the first TV sheriff who didn't carry a gun. He needed "nary a one." Maybe it only worked on *The Andy Griffith Show*, but Sheriff Andy Taylor showed that having effective leadership made it easier for people to submit to authority even in the tornado of town troubles.

Sheriff Taylor's leadership style was contrasted by his deputy's blundering attempts to lead. Deputy Barney Fife provides excellent seminar material for how *not* to lead. Barney's primary leadership authority came from the badge he wore with such pride.

John Maxwell points to this type of leadership as positional. Townspeople mocked Barney because he could only point to his freshly polished badge for authority. Barney was consumed with his quest for power, and the writers of the show frequently placed Barney in a position to lead when Andy was away. Of course a crisis was thrown at poor Barney in many episodes, and he was sadly ill-equipped to handle anything. His badge wasn't a useful tool in crisis management.

Leaders who boast of their positional authority have very few true followers. A mandate to follow me "because I'm in charge" will be met with vocal mocking. Today millennial staff members don't even try to hide their guffaws toward positional leaders. They simply point, laugh, and find an Andy to lead them.

Andy modeled servant leadership long before the concept entered leadership literature. Servant-leaders do not require titles, trumpets, or guns. Their power is ascribed from those who choose to follow. Andy's love for his town and its people was the secret ingredient to the show's success. Many organizations have a Barney on the organizational chart. Very few companies have a love-driven leader like Andy or Joshua.

> **Leaders who boast of their positional authority have very few true followers.**

I'll never forget Barney's response one time when Andy's son, Opie, got into a little fight: "Today's eight-year-olds are tomorrow's teenagers. I say this calls for action, and now. Nip it in the bud. First sign a young-ster goin' wrong, you got to nip it in the bud....Nip it. You go read any book you want on the subject of child discipline, and you'll find that every one of them is in favor of bud-nippin'....There's only one way to take care of it. Nip it. In the bud."[1]

Bud-nippin' rarely produces more than rebellion. A servant-leader doesn't need a badge.

> Jesus, knowing that the Father had given all things into His hands and that He came from God and was going to God, rose from supper, laid aside His garments, and took a towel and wrapped Himself. After that, He poured water into a basin and began to wash the disciples' feet and to wipe them with the towel with which He was wrapped.
>
> —JOHN 13:3–5

Servant-leaders are not weak. They love with great strength. Servants need very little from anyone but God. Servant leadership does not say, "Look at me; I'm serving." It is quiet, humble, and powerful in a crisis.

Love-Driven Leader
Truths to Remember

- A relationship with Jesus is the most important qualification of a leader.

- Leaders need to be at their best when the team is at its worst.

- The fastest way out of organizational crises is with high-level communication. Meet often, and talk a lot.

- Corrective confrontation builds trust.

- Leaders who boast of their positional authority have few true followers. A servant-leader doesn't need a badge.

Chapter 6

LEADERS ACT AND
KEEP ACTING

IT SEEMS THAT all leaders talk but not all leaders act. Love in action is critical for leaders to display. Leaders who take action demonstrate their core competencies, which builds trust among team members. A leader can "ask" a team for trust, but it is much better for a leader to gain trust by building his brand around actions that create growth.

If you think about the leaders you most admire, your memory bank is probably punctuated by "seeing" the leader doing things. Our warm and sweet memories about the leader likely center around actions that demonstrate the leader's competency.

It's not enough for a leader to walk the halls of an organization and proclaim his love for the team. *Lead* is a verb.

Consider the question Jesus asked Peter in John 21:15: "Do you love Me?"

When Peter affirmed his love for Jesus, the Lord's reply was simply, "Feed my sheep" (v. 17, NIV).

The command was for Peter to take action. Jesus asked the same question of Peter three times, and in all three verses Jesus responded to Peter with an order to act. (See John 21:15–19.) The central issue of the teaching of Jesus is love. Jesus clarified that Peter should demonstrate his love by feeding His sheep. With Jesus it was always about His sheep.

We see many examples of love in action in the Bible. One of my favorite examples is the story of Naomi and Ruth.

There was a famine in the land. Naomi's husband had died. Her sons had died. All she had left were her daughters-in-law, Orpah and Ruth, yet she was willing to release them to their destinies and walk through a bitter season of life alone. With tears and a kiss Orpah returned to her gods, never to be heard from again. Ruth had the same opportunity but chose a different path, the path of love in action.

> Naomi said, "Look, your sister-in-law has returned to her people and her gods. Return with her!" But Ruth said, "Do not urge me to leave you or to turn back from following you. For wherever you go, I will go, and wherever you stay, I will stay. Your people shall be my people and your God my God. Where you die, I will die, and there I will be buried. May the LORD do thus to me, and worse, if anything but death

separates you and me!" When Naomi saw that she was determined to go with her, she said no more to her.

—RUTH 1:15–18

Ruth demonstrated John 15:13: "Greater love has no man than this: that a man lay down his life for his friends." Naomi had nothing to offer Ruth, and Ruth had nothing to offer Naomi, except loyal love. Ultimately they led each other through hard times in the spirit of love, and the favor of God rested upon them.

> **Love *does*—it acts,
> and it acts consistently.**

Boaz, Naomi's distant relative in the land where the women sojourned, told Ruth: "I have been told all that you have done for your mother-in-law after the death of your husband, and how you left your father and mother and your homeland and came to a people you did not know before. May the LORD reward your deeds. May you have a full reward from the LORD, the God of Israel, under whose wings you have come to take refuge" (Ruth 2:11–12).

Ruth's faithfulness to Naomi put her in position to find favor with Boaz and ultimately see the Messiah birthed through her bloodline (Ruth 4:13–19). The story of Naomi and Ruth demonstrates love in action, but it does more. It shows the principles of the sustaining love of a leader. Love *does*—it acts, and it acts consistently. Love is not here today and gone tomorrow. Love-driven leaders see things through until the end.

The First-Step Initiative

There always seems to be an easy way out of anything. Ruth had a clear way out, but she took the initiative to demonstrate the love of God to a woman who had lost everything. How do we teach our teams to take this kind of initiative? Initiative is always available for the taking. Often our teams simply do not see what steps need to be taken.

Many workers wait to be told to take action to solve a problem. If a leader doesn't call attention to a problem, the situation is likely to remain in its current state. Perhaps action is not taken out of fear of doing the wrong thing. Or perhaps the worker has little training and really doesn't know what could be done to resolve the problem.

It is also reasonable to conclude that at least part of our team is simply too lazy to think and act. Some may feel it's safer to sit on the bench and wait to be called from their slumber. I recently read a devotion from *My Utmost for His Highest* by Oswald Chambers on this topic. He said: "But God will not give us good habits or character, and He will not force us to walk correctly before Him.... To take the initiative is to make a beginning—to instruct yourself in the way you must go."[1]

> **Love-driven leaders should teach the importance of a good start. The first step creates momentum if it is properly supported.**

The first principle a leader must teach about taking initiative is to make the first step. The hardest step is the first one. Naomi and Ruth took that first step together, surely leading and encouraging each other on a difficult journey. They started off on the right foot, and they ended up with blessings chasing them down and overtaking them. We are a nation of steps—twelve steps for this and twenty-one steps for that. The problem with steps is that many of us will skip to step twelve and start there. Step twelve is eleven steps too far. Love-driven leaders should teach the importance of a good start. The first step creates momentum if it is properly supported. I think one thing is certain about the process to achievement—if we skip steps in favor of a shortcut solution, we will lose the "best" of the process. If a process consists of foundational steps, when steps are skipped, the foundation is weakened.

Leaders must teach the importance of step one. Teach your team to take one action step immediately. I believe the Lord expects us to move as soon as His Spirit draws us. Following the lead of the Holy Spirit is not a "wait until tomorrow" thing. I believe God requires instant obedience. The Holy Spirit gives the nudge to take the first step—now. Drawing nearer to Him requires a move.

Orpah's Flip-Flop Leadership

Orpah had the same opportunity Ruth did to display God's loyal love to a widow and mother who lost her sons. But like some leaders in the face of important decisions she flip-flopped. She took a different course of action, and we never hear about her again. Orpah could not see beyond the immediate situation. She lacked a long-term view, so she headed in an opposite, perhaps safer, direction. Naomi and Ruth, by contrast, gave us an example of the blessings of laying down their lives for each other. It's not unreasonable to assume that Naomi and Ruth considered the path of Orpah. The three surely had discussions about what direction in which to travel.

Leaders who constantly change the team's course of action create instability and diminish trust. It's easy to understand why leaders can be influenced to change direction. Every point on the compass has a pulling agent. But I believe in most cases there is an optimum solution that represents God's best.

Most leaders operate in a crisis to perform. There always seems to be an urgency to produce measurable results. Now is better than later. The need to produce results can be the primary cause of flip-flop leadership. Today we are going this direction. Tomorrow we may abruptly turn and head another direction.

> **Leaders who constantly change the team's course of action create instability and diminish trust.**

In graduate marketing classes I teach the schism that exists in managing a brand. A brand manager is expected both to drive sales and profitability of the product and to build brand equity. In most cases these are mutually exclusive objectives.

To increase sales in the short term, many managers will drop prices and cut the marketing budget, which leaves less money available to build the brand. Alternatively if we develop a marketing plan to build the brand, immediate sales could suffer because of the time involved to build sales from brand building. Thus, a brand manager is tempted to operate in two mind-sets. But double-mindedness breeds instability (James 1:8).

Paul reminded Timothy to stay the course and to endure hard times. Paul didn't suggest that Timothy find a new direction. Paul told him, "If we endure, we shall also reign with Him" (2 Tim. 2:12). Leaders are tempted daily to change direction when results don't flow in as quickly as needed.

The "evidence of things not seen" (Heb. 11:1) is the ever-present concern—how we will build sales, increase the bottom line, or meet some other stated goal. Yet when we lose the "substance of things hoped for" (v. 1), our faith in God's ability above our own, we operate from our intellect rather than through the Holy Spirit. Certainly God's path for us has twists and turns, but His path is well lit. We need only to stay close to the Lord by seeking Him daily. We must depend upon the Lord to direct our paths. Our teams will appreciate a steady, patient path to the finish line.

The Role of Counsel in Choosing Direction

While Orpah went in tears back to her people, Ruth put everything at risk to follow Naomi with no guarantee she wouldn't be worse off than she already was. I remember one of my dad's favorite expressions about some of my loosely planned business ideas: "I wouldn't bet the farm on it." Since I didn't own a farm, I suppose this was his way of telling me that I wasn't likely to succeed at my plans. He didn't mean it to discourage but rather to advise.

Leaders need to be wise about receiving counsel. Not all counsel is wise or even godly. Even counsel offered by brothers in the faith should be filtered through the personal witness of the Holy Spirit. Proverbs 15:22 is very clear: "Without counsel, purposes are disappointed, but in the multitude of counselors they are established."

Spiritual leaders are gifted with a prophetic look forward for the organizations they lead. This might include vision for projects, market conditions, or perhaps even employee selection. Ruth had prophetic insight. She bet the farm and paved the way for the salvation of the world through the birth of Jesus Christ.

If I am seeking God's plan for organizational growth, the obvious methodology must include prayer and wise counsel. So wouldn't it seem obvious to seek counsel from men and women who hear from God and have active prayer lives? How can we expect to receive counsel from God from someone who doesn't pray, "Your will be done" (Matt. 6:10; see also verses 9, 11–13)?

If you have a question about the vision God has given you for your leadership, seek confirmation. Continue to diligently seek Him. God rewards diligence. When you seek Him, you will find Him. You'll keep the farm and cause it to prosper.

Loving Leaders
Transition Strategically

I mentioned previously that love-driven leaders see things through until the end. That doesn't mean they stay forever. When it comes time to leave a place, they must transition strategically because how they leave sets the stage for how they will enter the next season. Orpah left Naomi in tears, but was it God's will for her to leave weeping?

Man often gets in the way of transitions. Issues, preferences, and opinions muddy up clear waters. When God called a wonderful couple to be the new leaders of the church I was leading in Tulsa, Oklahoma, God showed me they would lead even before He showed them. I knew in my spirit whom God would set in place for the next season of our church as I left to serve at Charisma Media.

The kindle wood of transition is to know that God will sustain His work. The work was never mine. It was kingdom work, and God always provided. There was never lack.

When people began to talk about the church I had led in future tense, I naturally began to shake a bit. It wasn't easy to hear about changes that would be made and new buildings and new energy for growth. The flesh hurt. But in my spirit I couldn't have been more excited to know that our people saw that the work would continue after I was gone, and all would be well.

You may have led multiple transitions. This was my first. I'm not sure I led the transition as much as I just stayed out of the way and let the Holy Spirit lead all of us. But I offer a few thoughts from the experience:

1. Listen for the voice of God. I needed to hear the voice of God more than ever. My personal time with Him prepared me for what was to come. Leaders of transition must pray fervently for peace to prevail.

2. Journal. I wrote often about what I was feeling. In my prayer and writing time God was clearly present and comforting.

3. Don't let the transition hinder the flow of worship or work. We did our best to invite the presence of the Lord into every service and not let the focus shift to the transition under way. I remained mindful that our people attended church to worship and experience the presence of the Lord. To borrow from the story of Mary and Martha, man shouldn't hinder worship with table matters.

4. Hold relationships close. During the transition of our church leadership many of us spoke very clearly about what we meant to one another. We spoke about how life had changed when Jesus came into our lives. We spoke only words of life. During the entire transition we pro-tected one another with our words.

5. Let go. Thankfully the Lord had pre-pared a great couple to continue the work of the church. The best gift I could give them was to love them, encourage them, and stay out of their way. I have complete confidence in their call and their potential as spiritual leaders. They have made it easy for me to let go.

Someone told me along the way that if it didn't hurt to leave, I probably wasn't much of a pastor. I don't know if that is the metric that matters most, but it rings true in my heart. I notice now that my prayers still include many people from my church. I hope I never transition away from remembering always to pray for those I have loved so dearly.

On the flip side my father was in sales management for most of his career. I learned about sales by listening to him talk with his sales team. People spoke on a telephone back in his day. I'm thankful texting had yet to be invented so I could learn by hearing.

I remember on several occasions he had salespeople call to resign or say good-bye on their last day at work. He would turn to me and say, "Son, you learn more about the character of a person in his last two weeks on the job than in all of his previous days at work." I didn't fully understand his point until I experienced his lesson as an employer and as one who was leaving a place.

Leaving a job opens the door for more candid conversation. People will speak the truth more clearly. Some people will fabricate with great skill. The fact is behaviors change after a notice is given. Wouldn't it be great if transparency in the workplace occurred every day? The grapevine shouldn't be the source of information. Workers shouldn't be afraid to share their thoughts. Leaders should create a culture of open communication.

This sounds great in theory, but in practice our autopsies reveal multiple bites of the tongue. Many people who exit an organization leave because they feel "unheard." It's a leadership weakness when silence is rewarded over counterpoint. But the real leadership lesson is to teach your team the proper behavior for leaving a place.

It's not just about human resources procedures. Lead

the leaver into proper preparation for a spiritual separation. If God is engaged in the departure, order and peace will prevail. Christ, our example, is consistent. Hebrews 13:8 says He "is the same yesterday, and today, and forever."

Leaders love in word but more importantly in deed. They take deliberate action and leave a legacy of consistency and trust within their teams.

Love-Driven Leader
Truths to Remember

- It's not enough for a leader to proclaim his love for the team. *Lead* is a verb.

- Love "does"—it acts, and it acts consistently. Leader love is not here today and gone tomorrow.

- When taking initiative, the first step is always the hardest.

- Good transitions are well planned.

- Leaders need to be wise about receiving counsel. They should seek out godly people who pray often.

Chapter 7

KINGS DON'T
NEED TO ROAR

I'VE OFTEN WONDERED why God gave lions such a primal urge to roar. It's clear to all who observe the majesty and grace of the king of the jungle that an attempted leadership coup in the wild would be unwise. The lion has no need to proclaim his title as king. The proof is in the power of his great claw!

Leaders who roar demonstrate a lack of security in their calling. Verbal roars and threats to the security of workers have certainly been a hallmark of classic management. But through the lens of today's worker, roaring seems to be ineffective and weakens trust in the leader.

I once heard an expression about leadership in the military. One general said to a colonel who was soon to be promoted, "Never let your people think you are completely sane. Keep them guessing about how you might respond to any situation."

Today's work teams prefer quiet confidence from a leader. Overt reminders of a leader's title might indicate the leader believes only in her positional authority rather than her ability to generate influence. When leaders roar in a workplace to the point of needing a sanity check, something has gone terribly wrong.

My hypothesis is that leaders roar when faced with bad outcomes. "Maybe if I threaten their jobs, they will do better. Nothing works better than a good chewing out." In my opinion this is an impotent roar.

> For thus the LORD has spoken to me: Like the lion, and the young lion, roars over his prey, against which a multitude of shepherds is called out against him, he will not be afraid of their voice, nor disturbed at their noise, so shall the LORD of Hosts come down to fight for Mount Zion, and for its hill.
>
> —ISAIAH 31:4

Consider the kingship of David. Saul was insecure and anything but stable. When it came to competency and performance standards, David would slay his ten thousands, while Saul would slay his thousands (1 Sam. 18:7). Saul became jealous of David and sought to remove him from the kingdom by killing him.

David, however, was a man of covenant—a man of honor. Despite Saul's abusive treatment David spared his life more than once when given the opportunity to advance in the kingdom of Israel (1 Sam. 24, 26).

The ruddy would-be king entered into three selfless covenants with Saul's son Jonathan and stayed true to his descendants when he could have just as easily moved on and not looked back (1 Sam. 23:15–18; 18:1–4; 20:1–23, 42).

> **When leaders roar in a workplace to the point of needing a sanity check, something has gone terribly wrong.**

David consistently demonstrated leader love throughout his life, perhaps because he was focused on one thing. Psalm 27:4 tells us his heart's cry: "One thing I have asked from the LORD, that will I seek after—for me to dwell in the house of the LORD all the days of my life, to see the beauty of the LORD, and to inquire in His temple."

David's intimacy with God made him a stronger, yet quieter, leader than Saul. His need for God infused him with leader love. It began with his fierce dedication to take down Goliath. David didn't run out to slay Goliath with a loud roar. His weapon was his love for his people—the people hated by the Philistines.

Leaders Aren't Perfect

We all know David did not live a perfect life, yet God called him a man after His own heart (Acts 13:22). David loved God with all his heart, mind, strength, and soul, and he loved others as well. Although he caved into the appetites of his flesh when he had an affair with Bathsheba, he ran back to God when confronted with his sin, crying, "Create in me a clean heart, O God, and renew a right spirit within me. Do not cast me away from Your presence, and do not take Your Holy Spirit from me" (Ps. 51:10–11).

A lesser leader probably would have responded differently to the aftereffects of sin. Perhaps we would have seen denial, spin, or some baseless attempt at rationalization. Many leaders experience moral failure, but few confront the sin, as David did.

Consider David's infidelity as a metaphor for leadership. It's unlikely that someone wakes up in the morning and says, "This is the day I will have an affair." Leaders have a mission. Remember, David was on the rooftop watching Bathsheba during a season when kings go to war (2 Sam. 11:1). He was off mission.

Staying true to a mission is more difficult than planning the undertaking. Mission creep—that gradual shift in objectives—seems to set in early in the project. Shiny objects flirt with even the most resolved leader. The shift that takes us away from the narrow path of a mission is a subtle one. Leaders can become unfaithful to their purpose at any time. It is easy to forget who we are and where we are going. Fidelity to mission is often elusive.

An affair in our attention occurs when we forget who we are. It's not that hard to do. We are bombarded every minute to "look here" or "look there." "Wow! That idea is a real head-turner." In an instant, the blink of an eye, we can be tempted to forget the mission and jump on a new path. We think, "Our competitors are doing it; why can't we?" After all, we only live once.

I suppose I've been having an ongoing affair with my iPhone. It captivates my attention at times when I really don't want to go there. It gives me that "come hither" beep. I resist. Then it beeps again, and I forget who I am and where I am going.

Alexander Graham Bell never intended to create a tempter from his simple instrument of conversation. But Steve Jobs knew how to craft the telephone into a powerful tool of temptation. The iPhone is haptic, smart, and updated frequently. I question whether this technology brings me closer to my mission or further from it. I don't know if it helps more than it hurts. But at least I can read my Bible on my phone.

Fidelity emboldens a leader. Roaring into an iPhone or sending fire-throwing texts or e-mails only serves to scratch a leader's itch to be heard. There is no sustainable value in the roar.

The Anointing of God Is
Better Than the Roar of Man

The world craves a tall, strong, handsome leader. But God ordains a leader who is weak in the flesh. Spiritual anointing is coupled with gifts and a calling. Leaders are set apart for the work of their ministry. Once leaders are anointed, the opportunity for them is to remain fresh within their calling.

In 2 Samuel 3:39 David cried out, "Today, I am weak, even if an anointed king." Are these the words of a roaring king?

At the time he spoke those words, David had yet to claim his crown. He had a keen awareness of what he would become yet walked in lamentation about when he would sit in his God-ordained position. God's leaders walk in weakness of the flesh. While weakness before God is a good thing, it sometimes seems difficult to move a team toward greatness while demonstrating weakness in the flesh—when we don't know all the answers, can't respond to every challenge perfectly, fail to confront, or are unable to give every team member the attention he needs.

A strong, decisive leader offers his team spiritual strength while remaining weak in the flesh, lest he be tempted. God's strength shows forth at a leader's weakest points. Paul's glory came from his obvious physical weaknesses (2 Cor. 12:7–10). Our weaknesses qualify us to lead in God's strength. God blesses a weak king with fresh anointing.

Even in his weakness David made no excuses.

David had a powerful combination of heart and skill. All leaders need a similar combination of character and competency. It's been said many times, in different ways, that our competency will open doors for us, but our character will keep us there.

David didn't make excuses for his failure. A heart condition that tends to show up most when a person is under pressure is excuse making. When a leader offers an excuse to explain why a goal wasn't achieved, it's as if a bright spotlight is switched on. An excuse exposes the failure of skill and character. The leader receives two hits for the price of one.

> **David had a powerful combination of heart and skill. All leaders need a similar combination of character and competency.**

Leaders are accountable, and excuse making is a feeble attempt to deny accountability. Leaders who offer excuses fail to realize the long-term effect of accountability dodging. Excuse making from a leader is not much more than a roar.

Consider an alternative response to a failed project or missed goal: "It was my responsibility. We didn't achieve the goal. I learned that we should have been more aggressive in the first two weeks of the month. We put a new system in place to help us start better next month. I will get back to you with a report mid-month to track our progress."

This response does several things:

- It demonstrates that the team's failure is the leader's point of accountability.

- It demonstrates awareness of the goal. It's important to coach back to goals.

- It presents a plan to move forward. A leader of leaders isn't looking for blame but rather a plan to reach goals.

- It demonstrates a shorter term of accountability. When things aren't going well, shorter accountability checkups are comforting to all.

- It demonstrates to all concerned that the leader is at the helm and is aware of the necessary course correction.

The heart of a leader cries out for a team that welcomes accountability and is quick to adopt the skills needed to reach goals. David himself was accountable, and he was not shy about holding his leaders accountable.

The Roar of Victory or Defeat

For decades sports broadcaster Jim McKay could be heard on Saturday afternoons proclaiming these classic words: "Spanning the globe to bring you the constant variety of sports…the thrill of victory…and the agony of defeat…the human drama of athletic competition…This is ABC's *Wide World of Sports*."

I think Jim had it backward. There is so much more potential for agony in victory. And defeat can catalyze positive change.

Victories often lead to the celebration of self. Winning leaders can become independent of God and begin to roar, "I can do anything."

It is in defeat that we might be more likely to cry out: "Help me, Lord! I can't do this without You."

Man seems to place a lot of emphasis on winning and losing. Competitors on both sides of the field pray to win. We even use the label "loser" to describe those who don't measure up to certain standards or expectations. I don't believe the word *loser* is in the Bible, though the word *lost* is certainly a focus of the New Testament. Are losers lost?

I don't find the word *winner* in the Bible, either. Perhaps man-made labels don't translate well from ancient manuscripts. I'm reminded of David's second attack on the Philistines (1 Sam. 23:1–5). David had shamed the Philistines in a previous battle (1 Sam. 18:30), and at the time, he had recently been anointed king of Israel. The Philistines weren't deterred by their previous defeat; they planned a new attack.

> We cannot do what we've always done simply because we seemed to be winning. We must pray for a fresh anointing.

When he heard of the Philistines' planned attack, David went to the Lord in atypical leadership for a king and asked how to win again. Lesser kings may have attacked the Philistines using the winning strategy from the first battle. It's hard to change a winning game plan. But David waited on the Lord to provide direction even after he had won a sound victory. This is a model of leadership.

A roaring "winner" may have simply charged on ahead to certain doom, but David waited for the Lord to show him a new path to victory. David didn't bask in the thrill of victory. Victory can cloud judgment. As we span the globe to win the lost, we can't be dependent upon the way we have won other victories. We cannot do what we've always done simply because we seemed to be winning. We must pray for a fresh anointing. We need Him more today than yesterday. Who will tell the roaring winners they are losing?

David Was a Selfless Leader

David's loving leadership was sacrificial. He was willing to walk away from his kingdom rather than see harm come to his disloyal son Absalom. Another example of David's selfless love is he gave his men specific orders to spare Absalom (2 Sam. 18:12).

When we read or hear stories of sacrifice, the stories usually include some terrible loss of life on behalf of another. Somehow it seems to motivate us that one human had the courage to die for another.

In business we don't hear many stories about one business dying in order to save another existing business. Competition is known to be fierce and brutal, and the depth of sacrifice in leading a business may not seem significant in the moment. The return on investment of sacrifices made in business might only be revealed in the long run. It would seem to be rare that a sacrifice today will lead to increased revenue tomorrow.

There aren't courses in business schools that teach sacrifice as an important tool for young leaders to quickly develop. Students may not even hear the word *sacrifice* in a class during their college careers. But we know that leaders are often called upon to "die to self" when leading any team to accomplish a mission. The demand for a leader to make personal sacrifices is always present.

Leaders give up something of value to wear that mantle. Consider the sacrifices you have seen leaders make. What personal sacrifices have you made for the greater good of your team? It seems certain to me that all leaders sacrifice. The essence of sacrifice appears to be a matter of the heart. David cried from his heart, "The sacrifices of God are a broken spirit; a broken and a contrite heart…" (Ps. 51:17).

I don't believe a leader who demonstrates brokenness is one who is weak. It is quite the opposite. Roaring leaders aren't around long. It's the leader with a contrite heart and quiet confidence who enjoys completed missions.

As we consider a broken spirit to be at least one definition of sacrifice to God, we must look inside our own hearts to consider our degree of brokenness. Certainly leaders will be more effective when leading from a position of humility and with a contrite heart. A love-inspired leader's inner strength should not need to be a matter of roaring or engaging in public demonstrations of power.

An effective leader demonstrates strength through competency. Work quality speaks with quiet confidence about what matters most to a leader. I first must lead myself by expecting more of myself than I do of any team member. A contrite spirit shows through an outward display of humility in performance. Leaders produce results without trumpets and drums drawing attention. An effective leader doesn't require a duct-taped mouth to keep from roaring. There is no desire to roar.

Not needing praise is a clear demonstration of a broken spirit. I can do only what God does through me. When I get caught up in me and what I did and can do, I reduce my output as well as my leadership influence.

High-quality teaching is rooted in demonstration. We learn by doing what we have seen done well. Some leaders can only pass on instructions and commands. Effective leaders love to show and tell.

As I observe highly effective love-driven leaders, I am reminded that their powerful demonstrations of quality came with great personal sacrifice. They didn't achieve competency through a Google search. The foundations of their success were not poured with fanfare or in the presence of fan clubs. They sacrificed, put in the really hard work, and committed themselves to preparing for what was to come. Now their hard work and sacrifice make competency seem easy. They don't have to roar.

Love-Driven Leader
Truths to Remember

- Shiny objects can distract even the most resolved leader.

- Winning leaders can become independent of God and begin to roar, "I can do anything." It is in defeat that we might be more likely to cry out: "Help me, Lord! I can't do this without You."

- Leaders who demonstrate brokenness aren't weak. It is quite the opposite. It's the leader with a contrite heart and quiet confidence who enjoys completed missions.

- God's strength shows forth at a leader's weakest points. God blesses a weak king with fresh anointing.

- An effective leader demonstrates strength through competency.

Chapter 8

ROOTED IN PRAYER

I ONCE READ A quote that said, "We can't do more than pray before we have prayed, but we can do more than pray after we have prayed."[1] Prayer is the weapon of choice for effective leaders. Prayer must precede the steps of a leader. But after prayer, action becomes our mandate. Prayer is necessary but not sufficient. Likewise, action is necessary but not sufficient.

We see a powerful demonstration of prayer followed by action in the Book of Nehemiah. In chapter 1 Nehemiah prays the leader's prayer: "Hear the prayer of Your servant, which I now pray before You, day and night, for the children of Israel Your servants, and confess the sins of the children of Israel, which we have sinned against You. Both my father's house and I have sinned" (v. 6).

We know that after offering a prayer from his heart as a leader, Nehemiah set out to rebuild the wall around Jerusalem. Prayers for the wall to be rebuilt were surely offered by others who didn't build. But Nehemiah prayed and then took action. It was his love for the Lord—and His love for his fellow Israelites—that propelled him to prayer and action.

> **Prayer must precede the steps of a leader. But after prayer, action becomes our mandate.**

In 2 Thessalonians we read that Paul first asked the brothers to pray for him and to pray that the Word would "quickly spread and be glorified" (2 Thess. 3:1). After prayer he told them all to get to work: "For when we were with you, we commanded you that if any will not work, neither shall he eat" (2 Thess. 3:10). Prayer wasn't going to fill their bellies.

It almost seems facile to exhort a leader to pray before taking action. Yet I'm often reminded to pray a specific prayer prior to engaging in a very specific effort. Without prayer I act on my own. I tacitly declare my independence. But I dare not lead from a position of independence.

Prayer Precedes Godly Vision

During my years as a lead pastor I was often asked to share my vision for the church. Before people started asking me about vision, I don't think I thought much about it. I didn't pray about getting a vision for the church. I just started preaching and caring for people. I prayed for people and about their problems, but I don't recall ever praying for vision.

I began to feel convicted that I lacked a clear vision, so I fasted and prayed. The Lord was faithful to provide waves of thoughts about where I needed to lead the church. I first began to hear from God about programs and activities. The first clear initiative I was given was to provide bicycles for needy children in our community. Then came various other ministry programs and events.

In prayer the Holy Spirit also led me to understand that I was to grow in love for His people. It wasn't enough to be a teacher of the Word. I truly needed a pastor's heart. The Lord gave me a vision for action as a loving pastor. How could I lead a church without godly love for His people? I prayed for my heart to soften. I think my interactions as a Bible teacher were harder than my messages from the heart of a pastor.

I wasn't always successful at demonstrating love. My delivery could have been better. My face could have been more loving. I felt love in my heart toward others, but I know now that I could have demonstrated that love in much better ways.

So my vision of pastoral love was birthed in prayer, but the Holy Spirit continued to sandpaper my "program" mentality. I was transitioned to have greater focus on the individual. My mission was to love the people I was asked to lead—to love them as Jesus does.

After King Artaxerxes gave Nehemiah his blessing to rebuild the walls of Jerusalem, Nehemiah set out to survey the land. He took a few men—you might call them his core team—with him on the journey. After inspecting the broken-down walls, Nehemiah started casting vision:

> Finally, I said to them, "You see the distress that we are in, how Jerusalem is devastated and its gates are burned with fire. Come, and let us rebuild the wall of Jerusalem so that we will no more be a reproach." Then I told them that the hand of my God had been good to me and also about the king's words that he had spoken to me. And they said, "Let us rise up and build!" So they strengthened their hands for the good work.
> —NEHEMIAH 2:17–18

It's much easier to cast a vision than it is to secure buy-in and engagement. Many pastors cast vision for the ministries they lead during the previous year. Business executives remind their team of goals and milestones to be accomplished. Parents speak to their children about hopes and dreams for family unity and goals for the year.

Casting vision and speaking messages of hope are

not replacements for action. As we cast vision, we must be very intentional about securing buy-in. Gaining support for a vision requires much more than verbal approval from the amen corner. Pep rallies for the vision end at the point that work begins.

Why does a good vision from a competent leader often end in disappointment? Why is support for a vision often short-lived? Sustainable support is achieved with engagement measured by execution. Execution is what occurs when the excitement for a vision wears off. Getting things done requires much more than a desktop full of apps and to-do lists. Our teams must be filled with intention.

The job of a leader is to couple vision with intention. When our teams become intentional, progress ensues. Love-driven leaders create intention in an atmosphere of training. I may want to contribute to the vision but not know how to do it. Training is the single most important ingredient to execution. And vision becomes reality with execution.

Leader Love That Inspires

In the third chapter of Nehemiah we see that the vision was executed rapidly. The Sheep Gate, the Fish Gate, the Old Gate, the Dung Gate, and other areas of the wall were rebuilt. Nehemiah's love for God and for the Israelites inspired the people to work selflessly. With every task, no matter how daunting, I imagine their mantra was "I'll take care of it."

This mind-set is a fundamental of love-driven leadership. Mothers learn the essence of leadership from the first time they hold their babies. Moms know there is always something that needs to be done. I believe it was a busy mom who first said, "I'll take care of it." While effective leaders must certainly develop the art of delegation, careers are built by getting things done.

It's not just the busywork that gets done; leaders are focused on getting the *right* things done. It's easy to be busy being busy. But at the end of the day the story of progress is told by leaders who "take care of it."

The best surprise to a leader is when "it" is finally taken care of. An organization functions best in a culture of execution—getting the right things done. If execution is difficult in your organization, text a mom. Expect her reply to be, "I'll take care of it."

Just as Nehemiah inspired his brethren by refusing to come down off the wall, Alvin "Shipwreck" Kelly refused to come down off a flagpole for over three hundred hours in 1927. Afterward there were additional pole-sitting events and records set. Yet Kelly regained the record in 1930 in Atlantic City with a forty-nine-day stay.[2]

> **An organization functions best in a culture of execution—getting the right things done.**

Perhaps he had read about Simeon Stylites, who climbed a pillar in Syria in 423 and stayed there preaching and praying until he died more than three decades later.[3] Today the word *stylite* means "a Christian ascetic living atop a pillar."[4]

Simeon did all he could to escape the horizontal demands of the world for the vertical pursuits of prayers and private devotion. He obviously felt separation was the only way he could stay close to God without distractions. It didn't work out for the monk, as thousands visited his pole daily for prayers and blessings.[5]

As we compare Kelly's stunts to Saint Simeon's devotion and Nehemiah's determination not to come down from the wall until the work was finished, we find a clear principle of loving leadership. Leaders inspire. Kelly's actions said, "Look at me. I'm sitting on a pole." St. Simeon inspired people to find a closer walk with God. Nehemiah also said, to the glory of God, "I'm not coming down." Actions define a leader. Love is action.

While we don't know about the conversations St. Simeon had with those who came to him, we can conclude that he wanted to remain close to God and inspire others to do the same. Leaders take actions to inspire their teams. Sometimes the actions may seem grandiose or "out there"—or "up there"—but the shock and awe value of actions can set a team afire.

Inspiration doesn't occur with pom-poms and morning cheers. A leader charges a hill and inspires a team with actions rather than words. God calls us to come up higher. (See Revelation 4:1; 11:12.) Personally I'm not looking for a pole. I just want to inspire someone today, especially during these challenging times when opposition is rising.

Let this picture of Nehemiah's determination inspire you as it did the Israelites when they were rebuilding the wall:

> When Sanballat, Tobiah, Geshem the Arabian, and the rest of our enemies heard that I had rebuilt the wall and that there was not a gap in it (though at that time I had not erected the doors on the gates), Sanballat and Geshem sent to me, saying, "Come, that we might meet together in one of the villages in the plain of Ono." But they planned to do evil to me. So I sent messengers to them, saying, "I am doing a great work, so I am not able to come down. Why should the work cease while I leave it and come down to you?" Four more times they sent for me like this, but I answered them the same way.
>
> —Nehemiah 6:1–4

The enemies of Israel attempted several times to distract Nehemiah from building the wall, even lying to invoke fear. But Nehemiah wouldn't take the bait, and as a result "the wall was finished on the twenty-fifth day of the month Elul, in fifty-two days" (Neh. 6:15).

Nehemiah was focused on his commitment to finish the wall. Leaders are not distracted by folly. Leaders finish—and inspire others to continue to execute the vision even when everything seems to be against them. Leaders who take action and complete a work to the glory of God are fueled by love. If we care, we *do*.

When Things Don't Go as Planned

While Nehemiah 3 shows strong progress toward the vision of restored walls, Nehemiah 4 chronicles opposition to the rebuilding. Sanballat got fighting mad and started mocking the Jews—and Tobiah joined in the persecution. When that didn't stop Nehemiah's crew, Sanballat, Tobiah, the Arabians, the Ammonites, and the Ashdodites were "extremely furious" and conspired to fight against Jerusalem and bring chaos (Neh. 4:7–8).

Nehemiah's enemies fully intended to stop the work. Nehemiah didn't necessarily plan for such aggression, and it caused a distraction. He had to scramble to set guards on the wall and station people with swords, spears, and bows. He had to give them pep talks so they wouldn't retreat in fear. He called them to rise up and fight for the vision. Nehemiah didn't anticipate the fierce opposition, but he didn't let that stop him.

When things don't work out as planned, sometimes it is because our plans were based on faulty thinking. Consider these facts: Crime increases at the same time ice cream sales increase. We also observe that crime rates drop at the same time ice cream sales drop.

If we believed that ice cream sales and crime were correlated, we would plan to stop selling ice cream in hopes of reducing crime. We would hold meetings, develop plans, and launch a marketing campaign on Facebook. Unfortunately our faces would be wearing egg soufflé rather than gracing book covers.

Ice cream sales and crime are affected by the unmeasured variable of temperature in this example. There is a causal relationship between temperature and both crime and ice cream sales. The relationship between ice cream sales and crime rates is not causal. It only appears to be related if we misread the data. In this example we have common sense to help us interpret the fact that something else is going on with crime and ice cream sales.

This type of relationship is spurious. Spurious variables are not easy to see. In many cases this explains why things don't work out as planned.

Leaders command an action in the face of data.

Along the way an assumption is made that A plus B will cause C. When we get a wheelbarrow full of A, add it to a container full of B, and get nothing (or no consequential results), we can conclude that spurious variables are at work.

> **Vision includes seeing what might not go right and being prepared with a backup plan.**

Spurious variables are not easy to identify without testing. Testing becomes even more important when "everyone else" is reporting that a shiny new object is affecting the outcome of this or that. Crowds like ice cream, so I don't follow crowds.

What are we going to do if the plan doesn't work? Effective leaders have contingency plans. Vision includes seeing what might not go right and being prepared with a backup plan. I was taught this principle during my years in advertising. I had an intense client who was highly skilled at keeping me off-balance. He loved to watch me squirm as he tortured me with brilliant questions.

"I love this idea for a TV commercial, but what are you going to do if this doesn't work?"

"Sir, I know this campaign will work."

"It might, but what is your backup plan? Do you have another campaign ready to go?"

At that moment I wanted my mommy. I had given absolutely no thought to the possibility that a campaign might not work. A backup plan? We worked all night just to finish plan A!

I've been teaching the importance of contingency planning since that season of life. My client was correct. Projects don't always go as planned. I have faith in the Lord, but *my* ways are not *His* ways. I applied this principle in managing profit-and-loss statements later in my career.

Contingency Planning as an Act of Love

I became a big believer in lifeboat expense planning. It is simple contingency planning: if the planned revenue doesn't come in and we launch the lifeboat, what expenses will we allow into the boat? We have lifeboats attached to our ships because we love the people on board. Leaders who love will make plans to save the crew with the addition of lifeboats.

It's much easier to devise an expense-cutting plan before we need it. There is much less emotion involved. Then in a bad season when the captain calls for a lifeboat to be launched, the only thing necessary is to execute the plan. There is no need to make the hard

118

budget-cutting decisions in the midst of a crisis. You will be amazed at how clearly you will be able to think when a lifeboat is launched. And the team will adapt more easily when a contingency has been planned and previously communicated.

If the winds don't blow, make sure the sailboat has a motor. Consider Proverbs 19:21: "There are many plans in a man's heart, nevertheless the counsel of the LORD will stand."

When things aren't going well, effective leaders are the first to know it. A delusional, wannabe leader may never realize that the ground is approaching at an increasing rate of speed and his "plane" is about to crash.

Leaders develop a following because they have a trained ability to recognize the reality of a situation. Nehemiah didn't stick his head in the sand when challenges arose. I don't believe a leader is born with this trait—it is developed during times of fire. Crusty, experienced leaders with a full cemetery of buried projects have a strong sense of when a project is beginning a free fall. They have learned over time how to recognize the signs.

Nehemiah developed this ability on the job by the Spirit of God, and he modeled the way for others to learn and grow. Developing leaders too can learn to identify and correct a failing project. The next time a project underperforms, consider the following five points to correct the plan and provide training to your team:

1. "Be anxious for nothing" (Phil. 4:6). Pray for peace and wisdom to see the Achilles' heel of the project. Pray for all things hidden to be revealed. Pray for favor.

2. Look for the "one thing," the central issue behind the failure. It's there. In the course of failure fingers tend to point in every direction. Most of us expend way too much energy on red herrings. Real progress is made when we identify the core reason for the project's poor performance.

3. Find a change agent. The agent could be a tool, outside input, or perhaps even a new hire. Find someone with a vision for the forest.

4. Forget the long term. Engineer a short-term quick fix. Don't be afraid to use a bandage. Do something quickly to stop the dive.

5. Pay daily attention. It's not fun to confront poor metrics. Plan a daily

five-minute huddle with your team.
Assess the daily reality of the project,
and determine what your team can do
today to address the problems.

I won't suggest that "know when to quit" be added to this list. If God inspired the project, your mission is to complete the project with excellence. One other point to consider is the voice of the project leader. In the midst of severe turbulence on a commercial airplane the voice of the captain is reassuring: "Ladies and gentlemen, this is your captain. We will be experiencing severe turbulence. Check your seat belts, but know that we have been trained for a time such as this. We will land safely in just a few minutes." The voice of an effective leader should have a calming, reassuring effect as well.

Above all, contingency planning should be driven by prayer. We rarely have all the answers about what could happen. We have even fewer answers about what to do when the unexpected occurs. Yet when we seek God for answers, we find them.

I'm amazed but never surprised by what God gives me through discernment. Often His still, small voice leads me down a path I never would have considered on my own. I find myself making decisions I never would have made without the input of the Holy Spirit.

> **When we seek God for
> answers, we find them.**

I've often wondered what it truly means to be led by the Holy Spirit in business decisions. I've stopped asking the question and learned to pray more diligently about every decision: "Lead me, Lord, before I dare attempt to lead others." Loving leaders seek the voice of God.

Love-Driven Leader
Truths to Remember

- Prayer should precede all actions of a leader.

- Vision is clarified in prayer.

- It's much easier to cast a vision than it is to secure buy-in and engagement.

- Projects don't always go as planned.

- Lifeboat plans create stability in teams and should be created in advance, not at the time of crisis.

Chapter 9

LEADERS AREN'T LONERS

How many times have you heard the expression "It's lonely at the top"? I believe there is a fundamental problem with this claim. A leader who knows Christ should never feel alone.

A feeling of isolation or desolation should never overtake a Christian. The essence of our belief system is that God is with us. He came and dwelled among us, and now our bodies are His tabernacle. To feel close to Him, we need only to call upon His name and know Him as the great Shepherd. He never abandons us; He makes us to "lie down in green pastures" and restores our souls (Ps. 23:2–3).

But there is an additional troubling aspect to the expression that it's lonely at the top. A leader is only lonely if he is not a follower. Leaders have in most cases been excellent followers. They learned to lead by modeling other leaders.

When Jesus called His disciples, they had no concept of what they were getting themselves into. Simon, who was called Peter, and his brother Andrew were throwing a net into the sea when the Lord came with an invitation—"Follow Me, and I will make you fishers of men" (Matt. 4:19). They didn't hesitate to follow.

From there Jesus encountered James and John, later known as the "Sons of Thunder," while they were mending their fishing nets in a boat with their dad. He called them to follow Him, and "they immediately left the boat" and their family (Matt 4:21–22). Levi the tax collector left everything when he heard only two words from Jesus: "Follow Me" (Luke 5:27; see also v. 28).

> **The best leaders have spent time following and learned to love by serving a loving leader.**

Indeed, the disciples were quick to pick up and follow Jesus, but they had no idea what would happen next. They couldn't have expected that Jesus would one day utter the challenge of a lifetime: "If anyone will come after Me, let him deny himself, and take up his cross, and follow Me. For whoever would save his life will lose it, and whoever loses his life for My sake will find it" (Matt. 16:24–25).

Not only did the disciples follow Jesus through His miracle ministry, but they also followed Him through the storms. They followed Him when He was celebrated, and they followed Him when He was persecuted. Great leaders have a history of being excellent followers. The best leaders have spent time following and learned to love by serving a loving leader.

Demonstrating Christ's Compassion

Jesus was the greatest leader who ever walked the earth, and His disciples became great leaders by following His example. The disciples learned Jesus's language as they walked with Him and talked with Him. They gleaned from His words of comfort and His words of rebuke. They learned by watching as much as by listening. In the end they saw Him walk alone down the Via Dolorosa, the "way of sorrows," without complaint. Jesus loved and served consistently, even when walking a difficult path.

As His followers we are called to do the same. We may have positional authority, but we can't be averse to grabbing a towel and wash basin. We must be willing to get our hands dirty. Loving leaders know servanthood is not top down and function best in organizations where authority and responsibility flow horizontally. Service to one another is horizontal.

After a couple of long days of ministry the disciples were worn slick. They had been so busy they hadn't even had a chance to eat. Jesus responded as a servant-leader would. He told them, "Come away by yourselves to a remote place and rest a while" (Mark 6:31).

Such a response can come only from the heart of a servant. Leaders are never lonely when they serve with the compassion of Christ in their hearts.

To truly demonstrate Christ's compassion to their teams, leaders need to understand why people do what they do—perhaps understand others better than they understand themselves. If we can determine the tendencies of our team members, we are better positioned to handle behavioral issues that can hinder our team members, such as self-sabotage, the impostor syndrome, insecurities, fatalism, and a host of other blocks to progress.

Love-driven leaders seek to understand the behaviors that limit the capacity of talented people. We lead people, not robotic machines. We can't push a certain button and expect the machine to vend an excellent job performance. Some hard-nosed leaders will immediately dismiss the notion that soft leadership skills are necessary in the workplace. This type of leader sees the worker as expendable. "Produce now, or we will find someone who can," they would say.

The leader with a history of high turnover hasn't learned to do battle with the monsters that torment his work team. Rather than stand with a worker and fight through the foibles of gifted people, the option of least resistance is to find someone new with yet-to-be-discovered issues.

> **Love-driven leaders seek to understand the behaviors that limit the capacity of talented people.**

This is only a temporary fix. Leaders know to expect the unexpected from everyone on the team. People do not always behave rationally. You've probably said at one time or another: "I just don't know what got into him. He's one of the best guys in our company." The best leaders recognize behavioral aberrations as just that, aberrations.

When someone on the team is having his worst day, it's the job of a leader to have her best day. I pray for spiritual insight when I see something that is different in a teammate. I pray for understanding and grace to coach the person back to his strengths.

Carnal vs. Spirit-Led Leaders

"A double-minded man [leader] is unstable in all his ways" (James 1:8). A leader may claim to lead with the mind of Christ, but a carnally minded leader isn't difficult to discern.

The most obvious "tell" of carnal leaders is their focus on personal needs at the expense of others' needs. This leader displays little concern for those around him. He frequently displays jealousy for what others have and will openly mock their success. The carnal leader will habitually compare himself with others.

Carnal leaders will get angry over relatively minor issues. Their opinions are the only opinions that matter. They do not seek to understand others' views. This leader is driven by internal fears and therefore needs to control everything and everyone.

There are many descriptions of carnally minded leaders that fill volumes of books. The overarching truth about these leaders is that they are usually quite aware of their behavior and have no desire to change. They believe their ways are the right ways. Sadly many also believe they are spiritual leaders.

A Spirit-led leader is different from a carnal leader in almost every way. Consider these seven indicators of a Spirit-led leader:

1. Displays a continual flow of gratitude. A grateful leader expresses thanks as a matter of course. It is not a once-in-a-while thing. Gratitude comes easily because the leader lives in contentment.

2. Believes the best in people and knows there is a reasonable explanation for unusual behavior in others.

3. Welcomes healthy relationships. A Spirit-led leader regularly displays

the fruit of the Spirit: love, joy, peace, patience, kindness, goodness, gentleness, faithfulness, and self-control.

4. Demonstrates a teachable spirit. Spirit-led leaders display humility in the way they remain open to learning. They are avid readers and can learn from anyone at any time without prejudice.

5. Walks by faith. The "evidence of things not seen" doesn't rattle a Spirit-led leader. He knows with an inner peace that God is in control of every situation.

6. Considers the opinions of others but tests and considers the leading of the Holy Spirit above the opinions of man.

7. Has the name of Jesus forever on his lips. This leader speaks of the Lord throughout his day. He gives glory to God in his speech and is quick to invoke the name of Jesus in any environment.

People want to be around Spirit-led leaders because of what they have to say. A godly leader inspires people to come up higher. Their words give life to the hearers. They don't speak to tickle the ears of hearers but rather to exhort, correct, encourage, and build up. A Spirit-led leader is single-minded about his love for his team.

Insecurity is born in fear and develops into double-mindedness. Scottish writer Robert Louis Stevenson wrote a book in 1886 titled *The Strange Case of Dr. Jekyll and Mr. Hyde*. Today the fictional characters are often used to describe a leader who acts one way one day then behaves differently the next. Oddly the leader is usually not aware of the behavior and will fight vigorously to suggest he is the same leader in every situation. His delusions remain with him throughout his various transformations.

> **A godly leader inspires people to come up higher.**

It is fear that causes a leader to rapidly morph into someone who displays a temper or has erratic outbursts. Fear of failure surely tops the list, but fears such as health issues, relationship losses, and financial problems can further catalyze insecurity.

The clear and present danger of Jekyll-and-Hyde leadership is turnover caused by the leader's insecurity. When team members observe leaders responding to whims and emotions, insecurity develops throughout the organization. An organization guided by insecurity is slow to move, innovate, or respond to market conditions.

Team members are stifled. They stop sharing ideas. They find a box and hide in it. Bench strength evaporates. Favor is meted out in the organization based upon daily whims. Merit-based recognition and career development disappear.

Often a double-minded leader will display highly defensive behavior. An effective leader will be a defender, sometimes to a fault. The double-minded leader is inward focused, while the effective leader is focused on others. Secure leaders will display predictable behavior based on:

- Core values. Values have no wiggle room.

- Fact-based decision making. Everyone knows and understands why decisions are made.

- Having no hidden agendas. Everyone knows and understands direction.

Secure leaders offer high-level recognition. Employees are rewarded for known contributions, and feedback is consistent. Secure leaders also correct individuals privately. Team teaching is important, but correction is quiet because it is not meant to shame.

Love-driven leaders are Spirit-led, even when they

must make tough decisions. They operate with the mind of Christ during promotions and demotions. They ask, "What would Jesus do?"

> **Love-driven leaders are Spirit-led, even when they must make tough decisions.**

Four Leadership Lessons From John the Baptist

Consider the leadership of John the Baptist. First, we note that he was an excellent communicator, as is evident by the way John was introduced in Matthew 3:1–3. His message was clear and oft repeated: "Repent, for the kingdom of heaven is at hand" (Matt. 3:2). John the Baptist had many followers, and they all understood his powerful and convicting message. His clarity produced instant results.

Second, John was not focused on his personal image or how others viewed him. He wore camel's hair and ate locusts. John didn't appear to be the type of person who could energize a crowd. Yet he attracted the masses for baptism in the Jordan River. He did not lead with his external image. People wanted what John offered even though he didn't dress for success.

Third, in the face of visitors sent to determine what John was up to, he maintained his integrity and strong convictions. The Sanhedrin body of Pharisees, Sadducees, and town rulers came to the river to investigate John and do the baptism thing. He greeted them powerfully, saying, "Who warned you to flee from the [divine] wrath and judgment to come?" (Matt. 3:7, AMP). John made it clear that baptism would do them no good without repentance. He was not intimidated by ruling authorities. Yet we learned that John was ready to submit to Jesus.

The final point about John's leadership character is that he knew how and to whom to submit. He told Jesus, "I need to be baptized by You, and do You come to me?" (Matt. 3:14). Notice the radical difference in how John spoke to Jesus and how he spoke to the ruling Sanhedrin. Then John submitted to Jesus and baptized Him.

I doubt John had many formal classes or read books on leadership. Yet John was a definitive model of a leader led by God. John gave no room to the flesh. He didn't care what others said or thought of him. He did not suffer legalism but submitted to kingdom authority. The Holy Spirit will direct us to lead in the Spirit. I only hope this will not require a diet of locusts.

Creating a Leadership Training Program

A good leader should seek to raise up new leaders. A leadership training program is vital for every organization. So what is the proper curriculum for training leaders? A broad guideline is that content should focus on core competencies, character, and time management.

Every organization will have an approach to these topics based on its culture. Training should be specific rather than theoretical. Classrooms and seminars are the places to deliver broad-based "leaders should" training. The training should be designed to create effective leaders within the host organization.

Here are five questions to consider as you develop the content of your training program:

1. Who are the model leaders within the organization? Make sure candidates for leadership spend time with the right people. Think in terms of months rather than meetings. Effective leadership transfers through modeling.

2. Does the candidate have knowledge of the inner workings of every department in the organization? Create a rotation cycle in the training program. Decide how much time a trainee should spend in each department. Think months over minutes. Leadership training is not a spectator sport.

3. Does your company have a required reading list? Your training program

should engage trainees through reading. Leaders are readers.

4. Do you have a formal human resources training program? Be sure to include formal HR training in the leadership training program. Leaders need to understand the legal ramifications of every word they speak and every action they take. Recruiting, selecting, and hiring are key functions of a leader that require specific training in legal matters. Leaders know the law.

5. Does your organization have weekly training events? Trainees should cycle through the delivery of key training seminars. The future leader must develop advanced speaking skills, and a best practice is to train the trainer through active teaching. Leaders must show and tell.

The leadership training program should produce future leaders who know "This is how we do things here." But on a much grander scale the leader must be encouraged to improve her skills as a writer, speaker, and thinker. Strategic thinking is fuel for leadership. Leadership training is a process, not an event.

The Book of Proverbs is probably the best business

book ever written. It is also a primer on developing the influence of a leader. What leader doesn't need to be reminded of the following principles from Proverbs 27!

- "Do not boast about tomorrow, for you do not know what a day may bring forth" (v. 1). Leaders must speak cautionary tales. Certainly we must deposit confidence in the future of our organization, but we must do it in a way that demonstrates our total dependence on the provision of God. Strong leaders demonstrate total dependence on godly strength.

- "Let another man praise you, and not your own mouth; a stranger, and not your own lips" (v. 2). The speech of a leader is full of praise for her team. She is confident, humble, and smart enough to know that her success comes through the hand of God. Effective leaders are inclusive, especially when it comes to praise. *We* is a word that mobilizes a team.

- "Open rebuke is better than secret love" (v. 5). Leaders must confront. I believe the word *open* as used in this proverb refers to a condition of being open and honest with our teams. Open meetings are not the place for rebuke, but confrontation in private yields immeasurable benefits. Confrontation is information. An environment in which underperforming workers are given the silent treatment is like a petri dish full of mute bacteria. Unacknowledged damage perpetuates the spread of more damage.

- "Iron sharpens iron, so a man sharpens the countenance of his friend" (v. 17). Effective leaders make everyone they meet better. A countenance is easy to observe if only we take the time to notice. We cannot be so busy being busy that we miss the signs of distress around us. Influence is granted to a leader based on a relationship, not a title.

Jesus set the path for effective discipleship. He modeled. He showed. He taught. But above all, He loved.

Love-Driven Leader
Truths to Remember

- The best leaders have gone through a season of following.

- Effective leaders recognize behavioral aberrations and coach back to strengths.

- An organization guided by insecure leadership is slow to move, innovate, or respond to market conditions.

- Loner leaders often fail because they do not allow anyone to tell them the truth.

- Leadership training programs are a necessity for organizational sustainability.

Chapter 10

LEADERS LOVE
A FISHBOWL

THE CLARION CALL for leaders today is to become increasingly transparent. Those in the baby boomer generation seemed to accept the fact that leaders would tell them what they needed to know when they needed to know it. Their need to know wasn't as fierce as it appears to be today.

The apostle Paul was about as transparent as they come. He shared personal thoughts such as, "For the good I desire to do, I do not do, but the evil I do not want is what I do" (Rom. 7:19), and: "I am in a difficult position between the two, having a desire to depart and to be with Christ, which is far better. Nevertheless, to remain in the flesh is more needful for your sake. Having this confidence, I know that I shall remain and continue with you all for your joyful advancement of the faith" (Phil. 1:23–25). He even called himself the chief sinner (1 Tim. 1:15). That's transparency!

Trailing generations are cranky and demanding about wide-open leadership. The workforce today seems to have a need to know everything always—and right now, please. Transparency seems to be defined as, "Tell me everything you know the minute you know it." Our teams today seem to demand that every can of worms be opened.

I understand transparency to be something made visible by light shining through it. I understand transparency on a spiritual level better than I do on a leadership level. Does every work issue deserve to be lit up for revelation to others? Is it healthy for team members to know what I know?

At one time in my career I consulted with Jack Stack, author of *The Great Game of Business*. Jack is the founder of Springfield ReManufacturing Corp. (SRC). He believed in opening his financial books to all employees. The company held regular meetings to review profit-and-loss statements at a deep level. Each employee participated in profit sharing, so it was important to Jack for everyone to know the score of the game. There was more to his philosophy than that, but the notion of financial transparency was important to the success of SRC.

As I look back twenty years to when this type of thinking was popular, I see more downside than clear benefits. I've learned the hard way that a workforce can't handle some truths. We can't possibly provide enough information to lead everyone to meaningful transparency (full light).

I've settled on business transparency in this way. I shed full light on relationships with people. If I'm asked questions about personal job performance, I won't dim the light. If I am asked questions about corporate plans and activities, I will shed appropriate light. If I'm asked questions about business matters by people who are simply nosy, I will shed no light. Employees come and go in every organization. Some corporate information simply doesn't belong in the marketplace.

The Transparency of a Fishbowl

Light should reveal darkness, but every employee doesn't need the same quantity of light. Transparent leaders shed the right light in the right places. Everything matters. Everything a leader does is seen. The life of a leader is lived in a fishbowl.

A truly transparent leader doesn't care about the crowd gathered around the bowl, viewing every flip of a fin. Any leader who has led for any time at all is keenly aware of the viewing audience. For a true leader the fishbowl is a comfortable place to live. He does not regret living life in the bowl.

The beliefs and behaviors of a leader with integrity are instructional and faith building. It's likely that our behaviors have impacted people who observe what we do and how we do it. To gain a leadership role in an organization, a leader presents a track record of actions that indicate the probability of future success in leading a team.

Paul understood that life in a fishbowl begins long before a leader has any followers. An emerging leader has an instinct about how current behaviors will impact future assignments. Early in their careers future leaders choose to live under the brightest of lights, fully aware that everything matters. Even the smallest decision can and probably will impact future success.

> **The fishbowl is a classroom, a health-care facility, and a change agent.**

Senior leaders and mentors coach their young pups that leaders cannot hide. A leader is not entitled to a life of duplicity. A leader dies to self for the good of the team and the organization. Modifying *leader* with the word *servant* has always seemed redundant to me. Can you name a leader who doesn't serve? We serve with actions and observable behavior. We teach by how we live.

The fishbowl is a classroom, a health-care facility, and a change agent. The greatest changes in my life came by observation. Organizational health can be restored by the behaviors of a leader. As I think about the greatest changes made in my life, it is easy to recall the touch of a leader.

Be thankful for the opportunity to live an examined life. Everything matters.

Transparent leaders are often challenged with just how much to reveal to their teams on a personal level. Do we let it all hang out in a corporate setting, as Paul did? Our teams expect us to share all the good, bad, and ugly times. They want us to be real. While I don't believe my team needs to see me throw myself on the floor in a raging fit, teaching moments can occur in the course of walking out a challenge. Leaders have bad days. Things go wrong.

When leaders are transparent about their need to cope, trust is built. We teach others how to cope by how we model our coping skills. It seems true that a team reflects the actions of its leader.

Bad days are not simply about survival. We can teach and model how to thrive even on our ugliest days. Our teams will note our range of responses to everything. If my response is wide and varied, my team will lack stability.

I pray that over a long season of working with me my team will see controlled and predictable responses within an acceptable, narrow margin. I do not want my highs to be high or my lows to be low. I want to demonstrate a peaceful, relatively straight-lined wobble on the Richter scale. People tend to remember personal quakes in a leader's behavior.

I don't want to lose it. I'm too old to find it again! My go-to response in every rough patch is to refocus on vision. The thorns and heavy brush are not as troublesome when I remain focused on where I'm headed. I can't lose my *why*. When we lose our *why*, we lose our way.

People who throw temper tantrums have probably lost their why. If we can help others recover their *why*, we will often see a return of peace. So it's important for me to recite my *why* throughout every day. As I do, the Holy Spirit will lead me along the perfect path.

Love Confronts

Paul loved so selflessly that he wished he were accursed from Christ for his fellow Israelites (Rom. 9:3). There aren't many better examples of leader love than Paul. Yet he wasn't afraid to call out the Jews for their blindness and sin.

Paul loved the Gentiles so deeply he travailed in prayer so Christ would be formed in his disciples (Gal. 4:19). That's love-driven leadership—but he wasn't afraid to confront the double-mindedness that was leading them back into the bondage from which Christ's gospel delivered them.

Paul compared himself to a mother caring for her

children (1 Thess. 2:7–8). That's love-led leadership, but he was also quick to warn the church at Thessalonica about idleness and exhort them about the imminent second coming of the Lord. Surely Paul respected Peter, but he did not hesitate to rebuke him for withdrawing from the Gentiles in hypocrisy when the Jews showed up on the scene (Gal. 2:11–13).

Paul's willingness to confront sin prepared him for a life of evangelism. His leader love inspired him to pour out his life "like a drink offering" and rejoice while he did it (Phil. 2:17, NIV). Leader love cannot operate without a desire and an ability to correct. As the writer of Hebrews aptly said, "For whom the Lord loves He disciplines, and scourges every son whom He receives" (Heb. 12:6).

Paul's letters to the church demonstrate a great longing to lead his disciples into maturity and the character of Christ. We can learn plenty from the leader love of Paul. I know I did.

I'm reminded of a time when two of my former students spent the weekend with us. I was privileged to have taught them at the undergraduate and graduate levels. I was blessed to officiate their wedding ceremony and baptize the groom on the night before his wedding. I'm happy they have seen my life in the fishbowl and have chosen to remain close. During their visit a lesson on love was reinforced.

I've heard for years that some college professors develop gambling problems. The theory is that professors rarely see the outcomes of their work and become needy for the instant feedback gambling provides. Thankfully I don't need gambling therapy. And I've learned that all of my self-questioning about how "tough" I was in the classroom was a waste of time. Great students deserve demanding professors. Anything less is malpractice in teaching.

High standards must be a deliverable of any leader. A demand for excellence improves the future of the company. Young people who choose to be average will find their mean outcomes. Excellence isn't built on average performance.

During the former students' visit I reminded the young couple that their twenties are for learning and their thirties are for earning. (And their forties are for owning.) I want more for them. They know I will always demand excellence from them. They didn't come to me for a pat on the back. I believe they have never questioned my love for them, just as Paul's disciples didn't question his love for them despite his tough standards.

This young couple are focused on their relationship with the Lord, each other, and their careers. Their priorities seem right. Their path is well lit. I know I am not solely responsible for their success, but I'd like to think I played a part. Leader love doesn't need to gamble.

Demanding leaders see great outcomes. They are tough on standards yet tender with people.

Transformational Leaders Pursue Excellence

The apostle Paul employed the voice of a leader when he said, "Do not be conformed to this world, but be transformed by the renewing of your mind" (Rom. 12:2). Transformational leaders are first change agents. This type of leader is an enemy to any status quo scenario. Business as usual is scrutinized. The fishbowl reveals true change.

On the other end of the leadership spectrum transactional leaders impart direction "by the book." I'm never sure who wrote that book or under what rock it was discovered. I think it is an exaggeration to couple the words *transactional* and *leader*. Transactions are completed by managers. Not all managers are leaders, especially if transactions are their focus.

Transactional leaders fret about politics and coloring inside the lines. The Sanhedrin council seemed to include a gaggle of transaction makers. They led by rules. Jesus led transformation with love—and so did Paul. The Sanhedrin leader-impostors couldn't think a new thought. Transactional leaders lose sleep over change. Change threatens comfort zones and title-empowered incompetency.

Don't try to change the mind of transactional leaders. Their mantra is "This is how we do things here and always will."

The essence of transformational leadership is mind renewal. This leader asks many questions. Every question is a challenge to the old normal. Transformation occurs between status and quo. Quantum growth occurs within a disrupted organization. Paul's life, like that of Christ, simultaneously disrupted and transformed. Some folks just can't handle the truth of disruption.

As they seek transformation, leaders must operate as unto the Lord. That means keeping their minds in a constant state of renewal. Even in the face of the roughest disciples, their cry should be, "I believe; help me in my unbelief." Transformational leadership requires the fruit of the Spirit—it demands long-suffering.

> **The essence of transformational leadership is mind renewal.**

Paul said to the church at Colosse, "And whatever you do, do it heartily, as for the Lord and not for men, knowing that from the Lord you will receive the reward of the inheritance" (Col. 3:23–24). As leaders we must coach our teams to pursue excellence in every task they attempt. The best test for excellence I know is to ask, "Is this the best work you can do? Do you believe this work is excellent?"

Most of us have at one time or another felt as if *finished* is excellent. Sometimes we just don't do our best work. That's where a leader becomes engaged and does her best work. Leaders cannot demand excellence and expect to receive it as a matter of routine. But a leader can inspire excellence by work ethic, modeling, and consistency. Excellence is not a sometime thing.

Note what can be done to improve the work. Can something be done to make it better? If so, the work has yet to achieve excellence. "But I was excellent yesterday" doesn't seem to fulfill our calling to work "as unto the Lord." Teach the way to excellence. Model excellence. Inspire sustained, consistent excellence.

Teach Those Who Can Teach Others

The effect we have on others is our greatest currency as leaders. Beginning a work is not enough. Highly effective leaders—love-driven leaders—will nurture a team until it is mature and producing offspring. Love-inspired leaders replicate. Paul told his spiritual son Timothy, "Share the things that you have heard from me in the presence of many witnesses with faithful men who will be able to teach others also" (2 Tim. 2:2). It's not always easy, but leader love doesn't give up easily.

My wife and I watched a sandhill crane on her nest for several weeks on the golf course we frequent. We drove by on our golf cart at various times. She was always there and ready to pose for my camera. Most of the shots look the same because she didn't appear to move much. Then the rains came. A band of storms dumped over five inches of rain on the nest in just a few hours.

> **Love-inspired leaders replicate.**

When we went out to check on our crane, we saw only the egg on the nest. The water from a nearby pond came up high enough to threaten mama crane, and she abandoned her nest. Storms do that to people. "Thunder," "lightning," and "rain" can make us leave a project we've spent weeks, months, or years nurturing. Some leaders are simply not willing to die to self for the good of a project or a team in development.

It's not fair to judge the crane. Her instincts are to survive the day and lay another egg. But what about a leader who walks away when the going gets tough? Sometimes the flesh is weak and the storms are strong. Lead us, Holy Spirit, to finish the race. Help us hatch our eggs and raise up a generation of powerfully equipped leaders to follow our example. Influence has a generational impact.

Not long ago I read Bill O'Reilly and Martin Dugard's book *Killing Patton*. Bad reviews aside, the book reminded me of a classic quote from General George Patton: "Don't tell people how to do things; tell them what to do and let them surprise you with their results."[1] Well, the good general has one thing right in his thinking: there is a surprise coming.

I suppose the general forgot about boot camp, otherwise known as basic training. The essence of basic training is to teach men and women *how* to do what needs to be done. *How* must precede *what*.

Aren't you regularly surprised by what people don't know how to do? I truly believe that every business problem I have seen in my years in consulting and leadership could be traced back to a nexus of poor or nonexistent training. Leaders may speak about workplace culture and policies when acclimating new employees, but a vacuum exists in general in the teaching of *how*.

Remember Vince Lombardi's classic opening to his training camps for the Green Bay Packers: "Gentlemen, this is a football."[2] His first few days of camp—for an NFL team—consisted of blocking and tackling drills. How many games were lost in the NFL this past season because of miserable blocking and tackling? Most players know *what* to do but have perhaps forgotten *how*.

Our millennial leaders and those in development

learn from YouTube and Google. If we pay close attention to the training videos being delivered online, we will probably conclude that they were created to fill the *how* gap. YouTube has become a how-to library.

So leaders, how much time per week do you spend teaching the younger members of your team how to do what you expect them to do? Please consider the following six tips for training:

1. Put a premium on frequency. I recommend at least one specific training class per week. How would your ministry or organization be changed with fifty training sessions this year? Transfer the *how* to your team with sustained, consistent effort.

2. Review the basics. Teach blocking and tackling. Handshakes and eye contact seem to be a declining skill set. Start all training with the basic assumption that your team doesn't know the basics. And of course there's nothing wrong with reminder training.

3. Train the trainer. Leaders frequently delegate training to someone who hasn't been trained in the topic or teaching

methods. Invest resources in the development of trainers.

4. Adopt strategic curriculum. Certainly great libraries are available for training content. Be careful to review and edit *all* outside material. It's much better for the leadership team to develop and conduct in-house training.

5. Read and write. Reading should be a significant component of all training. Since all your team members could probably use writing help, I recommend a written assignment be included at the conclusion of every class. Ask open-ended questions, and review the content of the answers as well as the writing. My prophecy is that you will quickly see that training needs to happen twice a week.

6. Keep the Lord in the mix. What's a training session without a good devotion? Find a Bible lesson to tie in to every class. Pray for the Holy Spirit to teach the hearts and minds of your team members. The efficacy of your ministry or organization will ultimately depend upon know-how.

What Are You Thinking About?

Paul wrote in his letter to the church at Philippi, "Finally, brothers, whatever things are true, whatever things are honest, whatever things are just, whatever things are pure, whatever things are lovely, whatever things are of good report, if there is any virtue, and if there is any praise, think on these things" (Phil. 4:8).

Leaders often need to help their teams with "right thinking." When Paul exhorted the Philippians to "think on these things," his coaching demonstrated good love-driven leadership. Paul's list of what to think about included things that are true, honest, lovely, just, of good report, praiseworthy, and virtuous. The apostle's suggested thinking list is a good guide for a healthy mind-set in the workplace.

My guess is we've all been in offices in which one could observe the antonym of every word on Paul's list. Some workers assume the worst in all cases, and workers are sure to maintain a constant flow of words to describe their gloom and despair.

Love-motivated leaders create an environment for right thinking to stimulate growth. Healthy thinking is a catalyst for high energy and productivity. How often have you seen highly productive negative Nellys? The goal for leaders is to create an atmosphere conducive to an abundance mentality. Believing that God is in control and that His favor will prevail is a learned mentality.

The natural way of thinking is to grab whatever we can, any way we can, because "things are getting bad." The scarcity mentality is a belief system that comes easily. It's natural.

Monitor the prevailing wind in the office. One new addition to an office can change the atmosphere from one of abundance to one of scarcity. In the past I've watched one new hire destroy an abundant-thinking staff. A cancer of words is highly contagious. Effective leaders will drive out scarcity thinkers while constantly reminding all teams to "think on these things."

Though we value the power of the fishbowl, as leaders we will be quick to admit that as we look back over our careers, it is not difficult to find a suitcase or two filled with regrets. Even Delta Air Lines can't lose bags filled with "woulda, coulda, shoulda." I've long believed that Paul never fully released his baggage from the stonings he consented to or perhaps even orchestrated. (See Acts 7:58; 8:3.)

> And they threw him out of the city and stoned him. The witnesses laid down their garments at the feet of a young man named Saul.
>
> —Acts 7:58

But Saul ravaged the church, entering house by
house and dragging out both men and women
and committing them to prison.

—ACTS 8:3

Subsequent to Damascus, Paul probably lost sleep
over his leading of efforts to persecute Christians. We
have insight into his feelings from all his writings on
the mind:

- Ephesians 4:23: "And be renewed in the
  spirit of your mind."

- Romans 12:2: "Be transformed by the
  renewing of your mind."

- Philippians 4:8: "Think on these things."

Mind renewal permeated Paul's inspired writing.
But Paul wasn't the only leader who was tormented by
past decisions and actions. I think I have regrets even
about decisions I know were correct. Most of those
regrets are related to relationships. Good business decisions can end personal relationships.

"It's not personal; it's just business" is one of those
cop-out phrases that tend to be imbedded in leaders'
DNA code. It may be only business for the leader, but
most decisions have very personal impact.

Making the right business decision often leads to

regrets. Regrets tend to grow more irrational over time. We tend to forget the details of the issue but remember the relationship. The keys to the kingdom are found in relationships.

I'm thankful that grace helps me waddle through my regrets. But I've also learned that when grace is applied in the workplace, it is often confused with weakness. Though I see many examples of grace in the leadership of Jesus, I never have thought Him to be weak.

I've often applied grace in my church leadership. I've been asked, "Why are we still hanging on to that person?" Even in a ministry environment grace can be viewed as a weakness in leaders. So I also have regrets about not moving fast enough in making tough personnel decisions.

Even with a luggage rack full of regrets leaders must move forward with the confidence that they will receive daily bread. My God will supply all my needs today. As I pray believing, I know that the Holy Spirit will lead me beside still waters. Choose to make no room for regrets.

Somehow fish learn that a hand wave over the top of their bowl is their provision of daily bread. Fish swim and live in their bowls with total dependency on a hand from above. As leaders make decisions to impact an organization, they must know that God's hand is the hand of the highest and best provision.

Love-Driven Leader
Truths to Remember

- The life of a leader is lived in a fish-bowl, which is a classroom, a health-care facility, and a change agent. The greatest changes in our lives often come through observation.

- Leader love cannot operate without a desire and an ability to correct.

- Transactional leaders fret about politics and coloring inside the lines. The essence of transformational leadership is mind renewal.

- As leaders we must coach our teams to pursue excellence in every task they attempt. Have your team members ask themselves, "Is this the best work I can do? Is it excellent?"

- Love-inspired leaders replicate. Transfer the *how* to your team with sustained, consistent effort.

Chapter 11

THE PRESENCE OF LOVE

Hᴏᴡ ᴍᴜᴄʜ ᴏꜰ what is done today within your organization is motivated by love? Who will pray the leader's prayer? Who will invite the Holy Spirit to lead the way and the day?

Revivalist A. W. Tozer wrote, "If the Holy Spirit was withdrawn from the church today, 95 percent of what we do would go on and no one would know the difference."[1] What would we say about our organizations if we knew the Holy Spirit, who is love, was not invited in? Would things be different around the office? Would lives be changed in a meaningful way? Would the business of the organization operate any differently? Would people from outside of the organization think, "Something has changed around here"?

The Holy Spirit's presence in our organizations should be observable. We demonstrate His leadership in the way we treat one another, how we approach our work, and how we seek God. It is a simple sermon to preach concerning what *should* be happening within our organizations. If we are led by the Holy Spirit, everyone will notice His presence in how we do what we do. We seek direction from the Holy Spirit in our personal lives. Shouldn't leaders also seek direction from the Holy Spirit for leading an organization?

When leaders rise from their daily prayers, they should know that they've done their best to hear from God. There is no need to worry about what others think or do. The psalmist said, "Some trust in chariots, and some in horses, but we will remember the name of the LORD our God" (Ps. 20:7). All a leader needs is to follow the Holy Spirit.

> **If we are led by the Holy Spirit,
> everyone will notice His presence
> in how we do what we do.**

A revelation of leader love is written through Paul's description of what love is in 1 Corinthians 13:

> If I speak with the tongues of men and of angels, and have not love, I have become as sounding brass or a clanging cymbal. If I have the gift of prophecy, and understand all mysteries and all knowledge, and if I have all faith, so that I could remove mountains, and have not love, I am nothing. If I give all my goods to feed the

poor, and if I give my body to be burned, and have not love, it profits me nothing. Love suffers long and is kind; love envies not; love flaunts not itself and is not puffed up, does not behave itself improperly, seeks not its own, is not easily provoked, thinks no evil; rejoices not in iniquity, but rejoices in the truth; bears all things, believes all things, hopes all things, and endures all things.

Love never fails. But if there are prophecies, they shall fail; if there are tongues, they shall cease; and if there is knowledge, it shall vanish. For we know in part, and we prophesy in part. But when that which is perfect comes, then that which is imperfect shall pass away. When I was a child, I spoke as a child, I understood as a child, and I thought as a child. But when I became a man, I put away childish things. For now we see as through a glass, dimly, but then, face to face. Now I know in part, but then I shall know, even as I also am known.

So now abide faith, hope, and love, these three. But the greatest of these is love.

Each exposition in this passage is a leadership quality. So let's explore 1 Corinthians 13 in the context of love-driven leadership.

Leader Love Suffers Long

The older I get, the faster life seems to rush by. We're all in a hurry to get somewhere, do something, or speed through an experience. While we may be in a hurry, God is not. We live in a microwave generation, and speed seems to matter more than quality. But God teaches us the importance of time spent waiting. Waiting requires long-suffering, or patience.

Strategic leaders are results-driven. They want things done now, and they want them done right now. But Romans 8:25 speaks of hoping for what we don't see and waiting for it with patience. A love-driven leader is not anxious about anything but follows Paul's instructions in Philippians 4:6–7: "In everything, by prayer and supplication with gratitude, make your requests known to God. And the peace of God, which surpasses all understanding, will protect your hearts and minds through Christ Jesus." Love-motivated leaders bear with people in love (Eph. 4:2).

Leader Love Is Kind

Someone once said it's not paranoia to think people are talking behind your back if they really are. Prior to leaving a meeting early perhaps, like me, you've wondered, "What will they be thinking about me after I leave?"

Effective leaders are intentional about "back talk." Effective leaders have an instinct about finding something good to say behind the backs of their teammates. It's not that difficult to offer a good word about the recently departed. Regardless of what is said, we can be certain that our words will get back to the absent.

Perhaps someone has told you, "Pastor was saying some really nice things about you after you left the meeting." That's the kind of thing I like to hear. Keep the plaques, trophies, and certificates of appreciation. Just speak well of me behind my back. I will hear about it. Obviously we speak well of people face-to-face, but there is something very comforting in knowing the boss tells others good things about us. We all need to know that our gifts are appreciated.

In that same vein allow me to share a story from my work at television stations. I remember a general manager who wrote a personal note of praise about my work—to my wife. It was like an elementary school report card sent to my parents. The manager thanked my wife for allowing her husband to work the demanding schedule common at TV stations. The boss listed several things he liked about my work and stated how much he appreciated what I brought to the station.

Obviously my wife shared the letter with me and was so thankful to know her husband's work was appreciated. In my forty-year career I've received only one such letter. That person went on to lead with love in much bigger roles, and it isn't difficult to understand his success.

I suggest two action steps to demonstrate love: (1) find good things to say about others when they aren't in the room; and (2) write personal notes of appreciation. Write words of life. Leaders use their good words to encourage excellent work. Effective leaders are kind leaders.

Leaders Resolve Conflicts

A key responsibility of leadership is to teach team members to resolve conflict. All too often, it seems, staff members stumble into disagreement and lack the skills necessary to work their way out of difficult issues.

> **Effective leaders confront conflict.**

Does the following scenario sound familiar? Team members disagree. The two battle for their position. The meeting ends with no agreement. It's probable that one or both sides have taken offense. Both sides seek others to support their point of view. The issue may or may not surface again, but the offense will likely fester.

Effective leaders confront conflict. Be quick to nip offense taking. Focus your team on accepting the ideas and thoughts everyone offers. Let's not find ourselves discussing the same conflict a year from now. It's not a matter of who is right or wrong on the issues. The leader's focus should be on stabilizing relationships.

It's relationship building and maintaining that demonstrate our progress as Christians. We value people over processes. We care more for the people at the table than we do about their positions. We care about progress, but we know the source of our provision. People are the priority.

Leader Love Is
Not Puffed Up

"Yes, chef!" seems to be the only acceptable reply to Chef Gordon Ramsay's deep-fried rants in the kitchen. While I will quickly admit that television producers like to dramatize Ramsay's actions in a kitchen, it sure seems to me that his natural tendencies as a leader are fully transparent. I also know that Ramsay produces several of his own shows.

It would be difficult to find fault with the success of his restaurants. The Gordon Ramsay Group has, at last count, thirty-one restaurants scattered around the globe. He has earned six Michelin stars to punctuate the culinary success of his restaurant offerings.[2] He is a wildly accomplished chef and entrepreneur. He has also enjoyed success in television programming. Without question he is a star and a well-established brand. But I refuse to call him a leader.

I'm a fairly regular viewer of *MasterChef* and *MasterChef Junior*. I watched *Hell's Kitchen* a few times but could not endure seeing the chef brutally criticize the contestants. The show has an appropriate title for the leadership style Ramsay displays. Ramsay behaves like a brat and has zero control of his language. If he stopped the flinging of expletives, would his food taste bad or his shows become boring? Would his brand be diminished?

It's not unusual for a chef to "lose it" the way Ramsay does. Bad behavior is usually understood and even expected in a hot kitchen. Many would-be chefs can't take the heat, so they prefer to stay out of such kitchens. The creative ability, artistry, and chemistry of a master chef seem to allow a margin for tantrum throwing. It goes with the territory.

All the good Ramsay does is tainted by the way we see him treat people. A fundamental principle of leadership is to nurture and grow a team of future leaders. The more established a leader's brand becomes, the more important it is to demonstrate controlled aggression in the heat of battle. A fast-paced, working kitchen certainly isn't the place for low-confidence line cooks.

But we must expect more of leaders. All leaders swim in a fishbowl. Future stars keep one eye on the skillet and another eye on the style of a leader. A future master chef might watch Ramsay and think, "Maybe Gordon's style of leadership is how I should run my kitchen."

I think this is what bothers me most about watching Ramsay throw a fit as he kicks neophytes out of his kitchen. Young people model what appears to be successful behavior. But the untold stories of chefs who have failed in abusive kitchens provide a multipage menu of how not to lead. Gordon Ramsay is truly a master chef and businessman. But in my opinion this guy represents all that is bad about leaders with no followers. No, chef!

Your gifts open doors. Your character keeps you there. Luke 14:11 reminds us, "For whoever exalts himself will be humbled, and he who humbles himself will be exalted."

Leader Love Doesn't Behave Poorly

The potential for a leader to become toxic when working with others grows as a function of time. The longer a leader serves the same group of followers, the more likely it is that a bully will appear.

New leaders usually enter the organization with a servant's attitude and a nice dose of humility. Over time a leader's success can lead to the development of narcissism and the onset of bullying. Sycophants feed the bully, and the atmosphere for toxic leadership can grow and fester.

Many workers have had to contend with a bully-boss. A workplace bully can come in different sizes and shapes. A bully usually lives in a fantasy world accented by ambivalence and hypocrisy. The favorite weapons of a bully are threatening behavior, public humiliation, and tantrum throwing. Various forms of ostracism are also used.

Love-driven leaders will constantly review their personal behavior. The quickest cure for bullying activities is for the leader to take long looks into a reflecting pond. A mirror will do in a pinch. But ponds are better for a quick refresher course.

Look for the appearance of any of these signs as an indicator it may be time for repentance: intimidation (Jesus taught meekness), shouting (Jesus healed with a whisper), name calling (Jesus called us children), cruel sarcasm (this violates the Ephesians 4:29 rule), or stealing credit (Jesus loved the back of the line).

We know that hurting people hurt people. Hurting leaders have inherent power to hurt many. Toxic leadership begins in the heart. Leaders, pray that the condition of your heart will be revealed. Duplicitous behavior is rarely accidental. Thankfully relief from toxic behavior is available through Christ.

Leader Love Is
Not Easily Provoked

When Martha mixed a spoonful of mood into her service bowl, she became less effective, and Jesus called her out on it. "Martha, Martha, you are anxious and troubled about many things" (Luke 10:41). Jesus called Martha into a deeper relationship with Himself, while Mary sat mood-less at the feet of the Lord.

Anxiety is expressed in moodiness. It gets in the way of spiritual and marketplace progress. Anxiety marks an independent person. When we draw close to Jesus, we don't need a mood ring.

Leaders do not have the luxury of being in a mood. Most of us have asked, "Is it safe to go visit with the boss? What kind of mood is he in today?" Love-driven leaders strive for consistency. Precision is the goal. A key ingredient to quality decision making is objectivity. Perhaps how we feel about an issue is the cause of mood changes. Good thinking crashes a mood party. Clear thinking is unaffected by feelings.

Leader Love
Thinks No Evil

One of my favorite proverbs is "A word fitly spoken is like apples of gold in settings of silver" (Prov. 25:11). I suppose I will always be learning to apply this verse.

I seem to specialize in finding ways to say the wrong thing at the wrong time. My sense of what is funny is often not funny to hearers. It certainly doesn't pass the Ephesians 4:29 test: "Let no unwholesome word proceed out of your mouth, but only that which is good for building up, that it may give grace to the listeners."

The language of a leader can improve instantly by his simply using the Ephesians filter and asking himself, "Will these words build up?" I believe bad thinking leads to bad speaking. Leaders often speak into situations based on what they have been told or perhaps read in an e-mail. The challenge is *not* to jump quickly into any thought.

When presented with news about a team member or work issue, leaders must be careful to think about the news with spiritual guidance. Problems deepen when a leader thinks, "Here we go again," or, "It's just Fred being Fred." Fatalistic thinking is what eventually catalyzes acid tongue disease.

The Holy Spirit will lead us to think purer thoughts. We will hear bad news but think good thoughts. We will actively seek the most reasonable explanation about what we hear. We will form a spiritual opinion about what we hear while closing all doors to evil interpretation. The Spirit of God will provide discernment in a matter, but the Spirit will also lead us to speak restoration rather than destruction. "A word fitly spoken" springs forth from spiritually disciplined thinking.

Leader Love
Rejoices in Truth

Many leaders have a low awareness of their personal strengths. Not surprisingly leaders seem to be much more aware of their weaknesses. Much has been written on the topic of strength finding. The famed management consultant Peter Drucker wrote that the most important thing we can know about ourselves is our personal strengths.[3]

> **Many leaders operate in what they *want* their strengths to be. But when we work outside of our strengths, we have little peace.**

The use of a leader's strengths can catalyze change in an organization. Any sort of focus on weaknesses has little impact on the person or the organization. Yet this thinking doesn't always transfer from the leader to the worker. If we conduct a content analysis on performance reviews, we will find much more emphasis on employee weaknesses than strength building.

I believe that God gave us the gifts and anointing

to perform with excellence in the place in which we are planted. The problem is that many of us fail to recognize our strengths, and therefore we do not operate within them. In my observation, many leaders operate in what they *want* their strengths to be. But when we work outside of our strengths, we have little peace. We exert effort and struggle. We gnash teeth.

Drucker believed that the Jesuits, a Catholic order founded by St. Ignatius Loyola, and the Calvinists, a Protestant Reform movement founded by John Calvin—both started in the mid-sixteenth century—developed a very valuable technique called "feedback analysis" to help their priests and ministers find their strengths and grow into what they were called to be.

Drucker wrote:

> Whenever a Jesuit priest or a Calvinist pastor does anything of significance (for instance, making a key decision), he is expected to write down what results he anticipates. Nine months later, he then feeds back from the actual results to these anticipations....I have followed this method myself now for fifty years. It brings out what one's strengths are—and this is the most important thing an individual can know about himself or herself. It brings out where improvement is needed and what kind of improvement is needed. Finally, it brings out what an individual

> cannot do and therefore should not even try to do. To know one's strengths, to know how to improve them, and to know what one cannot do—they are the keys to continuous learning.[4]

Feedback analysis provides valuable insight. In the last year I made journal notes of key decisions as I made them. I'm just now understanding the impact of those decisions and adjusting my thinking accordingly. I clearly see areas of strength and weakness. Feedback analysis provides evidence of strengths. There is little emotional bias in historical review. Facts seem to preach good sermons. Our personalities may push us forward into a project, but it's our strengths that will propel success.

Leaders will do best when they find their lane and work in it. The Holy Spirit will lead us. We just need to learn to listen to His voice. I take comfort in the fact that He knows me best.

Leader Love Bears, Believes, Hopes, and Endures

Our success at pushing through any difficulty is a function of our mind-set. Solomon explains, "For as he thinks in his heart, so is he" (Prov. 23:7). Hope, perseverance, and faith live or die in how we think about our teams and our projects.

God created us to be creative. He created us in His image. Many people believe that only certain people are given the gift of creativity. I do not believe this. God created His people to look at every day with vision. The Spirit of God, which dwells within us, helps us to see the possibilities in everything. As we look at the people we lead, we see what God is doing and will do with them.

In general people aren't feeling very creative these days. However, we don't walk by feelings, and creativity is not fueled by feelings. We are born to create. I believe everyone can be taught to create on demand. Leaders can and should teach creativity. It can be as simple as allowing people to stumble through their projects. Don't solve every problem your team faces. Struggles encourage creative solutions.

When things stop working the way things have always worked, it's a great time to encourage something new. God has gifted you to create. When we empower people to be creative, of course we must make room for their mistakes.

Although God never makes mistakes, the rest of us can and do. Many of us frequently admit, "We all make mistakes." And we say, "To err is human," and, "If you're not making mistakes, then you aren't doing anything."

Leaders will usually fall into one of two camps when it comes to their culture of creativity: (1) they will discourage mistakes and respond in a punitive manner, or

(2) they will encourage mistakes that occur through efforts to innovate and respond in an encouraging manner.

I believe we are influenced by the managers we served early in our careers. Much like parenting scripts, we tend to believe what we hear from our bosses as we launch out in our first few jobs. So our mistake tolerance is well established in the early steps along our career paths.

In growing healthy organizations, love leaders establish a culture that encourages trial and error. If we want our teams to be creative, we cannot discourage the fruit of a creative thought. Apparent mistakes may eventually prove to be long-term winners.

Put another way, we must avoid the mortification of mistakes. I know I've questioned myself a few hundred times along the way, but I've tried not to beat myself up for more than a short pity party. I've learned to expect mistakes. I don't ever like a mistake, but I know that blunders and brilliance are kissing cousins.

Confronting Poor Performance in Love

One of the most difficult yet necessary responsibilities of a leader is providing proper correction to his team. Confronting poor performance is not pleasant. Unfortunately our training in healthy confrontation methods probably came at the hands of a leader who was also not trained to properly confront. We aren't born with a genetic code to help us handle poor performance within our teams. Often the path of least resistance is the path most traveled.

I still remember Kenneth Blanchard and Spencer Johnson's book *The One Minute Manager*[5] and highly recommend it to new managers. Drawing from Blanchard, I've developed a system for performance improvement that is simple and effective:

- Praise in public; correct in private. (Why do so many leaders have this backward?)

- Surround a corrective statement with several positive statements. I've always tried to use the Whopper formula—bread, bread, meat, bread, bread; positive, positive, improve this, positive, positive.

- Coach back to goals.

- Use questions.

Consider this example:

Manager: What is our goal (or standard) for cleaning tables after a guest leaves our restaurant?

Team member: To bus a table within ninety seconds of a guest leaving the table.

Manager: What do you see in the dining room?

Team member: A lot of messy tables.

Manager: What needs to happen for us to achieve our goal?

While this discussion may appear to be simplistic, the fact is, we need to have more simplistic discussions with our teams relative to goal achievement. Maintaining standards is an important marker for goal achievement. Repeat the goals. Repeat expectations. Confront with questions.

Here's another example:

Pastor: What is our goal for sending follow-up notes to visitors?

Staff: We want a note in their mailbox by the Wednesday after their visit.

Pastor: When is the last time we mailed visitor notes?

Staff: I don't remember the last time we sent a card.

Pastor: Did the goal change?

Staff: No.

Pastor: What needs to happen for us to achieve our goal?

I think we would all agree this exchange was confrontational, but it wasn't mean-spirited, humiliating, or fault-finding. The volume of the leader's voice will not change the team member's answers. Passive aggression won't bring us a step closer to the goal. Confront the issue with two powerful questions: "What is our goal?" and "What needs to happen to achieve our goal?" Effective leaders are tender with people but tough on standards.

Paul's great love chapter reminds us that love leaves a trail. As we lead in the presence of the Holy Spirit, we love as we breathe. If love is not present in our daily interactions, surely we aren't walking in the presence of God. God is love. How can we lead without acting in love?

Love-Driven Leader
Truths to Remember

- Love-driven leaders find something good to say behind the backs of their teammates.

- A key responsibility of leadership is to teach team members to resolve conflict.

- Loving leaders don't allow their staff members to battle for their favor.

- Our gifts open doors. Our character keeps us there.

- Love-driven leaders confront team members with questions, not condemnation.

Chapter 12

THE GOLDEN RULE
OF LEADERSHIP

Jesus taught us to "do unto others as you would have others do unto you" (Luke 6:31). I think more is required of leaders whose goal is to serve rather than be served. We must certainly model this teaching but also find ways to expand the directive. Effective leaders do more than the minimum.

It seems minimal to me to simply treat people the way I want to be treated. If I am a servant-leader, I don't need or require much. The people we serve should be treated better than we expect to be treated. I'm suggesting a leader's standard should be to treat others better than we would ever expect to be treated. It's not difficult to see that Jesus did much more than the minimum. I want to lead people by finding ways to do more for them than they would ever expect.

In short, I want to lead like Jesus.

Jesus loved people as no other leader could. He spoke as one with authority as He spoke life into those on His path. But Jesus did more. He was also a teacher.

Modeling is powerful, but Jesus showed us that leaders can do better than basic modeling. We can teach with our words. We can teach our teams how to treat people better than they would want to be treated. It's not enough for me to love those I lead. I must teach my team to grow in love for others.

This can be a difficult task. Our teams often comprise hurting people. It's likely many of the people we lead don't know how to treat others because of their own personal baggage. We must show them that the standard for service shouldn't be our own expectations. Rather, we help others without consideration of our own needs.

You are equipped to do this because when you accepted Jesus as Savior, you accepted Him as Lord, meaning you accepted Him as your leader. When you submit to His leadership, you receive grace, wisdom, mercy, and everything else you need to accomplish what He has called you to do.

> **Love-driven leaders are excellent followers of the ultimate love-driven leader.**

God always causes us to triumph in Him (2 Cor. 2:14). When Jesus ascended to heaven, the Father sent the Holy Spirit to lead us and guide us (John 16:13). Jesus also sent "apostles, prophets, evangelists, pastors, and teachers" to equip us for ministry work (Eph. 4:11–12), and He has set in place authorities in the earth (Rom. 13:1).

Love-driven leaders are excellent followers of the ultimate love-driven leader. Even Jesus was a follower. He told His disciples, "Truly, truly I say to you, the Son can do nothing of Himself, but what He sees the Father do. For whatever He does, likewise the Son does" (John 5:19).

A leader who is led by love understands authority structures. The centurion in Matthew 8 had such a clear understanding of authority it caused Jesus to marvel. When Jesus agreed to journey to the official's home to heal the man's servant, the centurion said:

> Lord, I am not worthy that You should come under my roof. But speak the word only, and my servant will be healed. For I am a man under authority, having soldiers under me. And I say to this man, "Go," and he goes, and to another, "Come," and he comes, and to my servant, "Do this," and he does it.
>
> —MATTHEW 8:8–9

The centurion understood chain of command, and so must we because at the core of leader love is submission to the authority of Christ. The only way we can demonstrate the golden rule of leadership is if we follow Christ. "What would Jesus do?" should be top of mind for leaders seeking to operate in the law of love, whether that's in everyday meetings, in confrontations, or in other matters of leading. Asking this question will help us understand how Christ led and how the Holy Spirit is leading us.

Fear God, Not Man

To truly model Jesus's leadership, we must care more about our innermost spiritual condition than our outward appearance. Jesus taught us to focus on the authentic self rather than some contrived exterior image. Jesus did not try to impress people. He spoke hard sayings and often withdrew from His followers into a desert place for prayer. He challenged the self-righteous. Jesus wasn't concerned with His public persona.

Jesus said things such as: "Do not fear those who kill the body but are not able to kill the soul. But rather fear Him who is able to destroy both soul and body in hell" (Matt. 10:28). In other words, fear God and not man. Proverbs 29:25 says, "The fear of man brings a snare, but whoever puts his trust in the LORD will be safe."

We see a devastating example of this in Saul's ministry. Through the prophet Samuel the Lord told Saul, Israel's first king, to go and utterly destroy the Amalekites—and everything they had. The Lord was crystal clear: "Do not have compassion on them but put to death both man and woman, child and infant, ox and sheep, camel and donkey" (1 Sam. 15:3).

Saul set out to execute the Lord's strategy and started well. He struck the Amalekites from Havilah to Shur. But he took Agag, the king of the Amalekites, alive. Saul also spared the best of the sheep, fatlings, and lambs. This grieved the Lord and Samuel. When Samuel confronted Saul, he argued with the man of God about his actions before finally exposing the fear of man in his heart:

> I have sinned. For I have transgressed the commandment of the LORD, and your words, because I feared the people, and obeyed their voice. Now therefore, please pardon my sin and return with me, that I may worship the LORD.
>
> —1 SAMUEL 15:24–25

There's a leadership lesson here. Often leaders fail to do the right thing because they care more about being liked than about being principled. Some leaders consider their "company image" before saying or doing things that are correct but unpopular. That isn't the example Jesus set.

Our spiritual image is developed "precept upon precept, precept upon precept, line upon line, line upon line, here a little, there a little" (Isa. 28:10). The spiritual nips and tucks are not plastic. Plastic things are not eternal.

> **Often leaders fail to do the right thing because they care more about being liked than about being principled.**

How Jesus Handled Dropped Balls

One of the most difficult yet important opportunities to demonstrate leader love as Jesus did is when a team member doesn't do what is expected. A leader's character is tested in the fire of poor execution from a work team. How do we love those who don't, can't, or simply won't do things right? How did Jesus handle poor performance?

His instruction was simple: "Sit here while I pray" (Mark 14:32). The time was at hand for Jesus. At Gethsemane He needed to pray and asked a few disciples to keep watch: "Then He came and found them sleeping and said to Peter, 'Simon, are you sleeping? Could you not keep watch one hour?'" (Mark 14:37).

Many leaders have asked similar questions: "Didn't you know I needed this today?" "How many times do I have to explain this to you?" "When can I expect the report I needed yesterday?"

It's the not doing the simple things that causes leaders the greatest headaches. It's frustrating to see the same mistakes made daily. It's even more frustrating to see simple things missed or left undone. How did Jesus handle His followers when they could not even stay awake as He asked?

1. He confronted them with questions: "Are you sleeping? Could you not keep watch one hour?" (Mark 14:37). A third set of questions is implied in Mark 14:40: "And they did not know what to answer Him."

2. He repeated the instructions and confronted each failure with questions.

3. He led them forward, saying, "Rise up, let us go" (Mark 14:42).

Sometimes the best response is to gather the team and take action together. Any leader could have simply moved on alone from Gethsemane. Jesus could have terminated the employment of His prayer team. He could have issued a stern lecture and received promises such as, "This won't ever happen again, boss."

Jesus's decision to simply gather His team and move on is inspiring. My guess is the disciples felt terrible about their inability to do as their Lord requested. Jesus had much more on His mind and knew His action was the best response. Seeing Judas nearby also helped Jesus move His team along.

Jesus knew that His disciples had willing spirits;

their hearts were good. Sadly their flesh won the battle in the garden. Effective leaders know that people have bad days. The response of a leader to weak flesh should closely resemble the leadership of Jesus. Confront. Question. Act.

Three Things Jesus Teaches Us About Meetings

Jesus made the most of His time with His team members. He taught them with every choice He made, but He also set aside specific times to meet with them. Jesus's meetings were always effectual, and we can learn much from Him about conducting productive meetings.

The key to making sure meetings are not a waste of time is to keep the meeting action focused on specific teaching. When Jesus called His chosen disciples up to the mountain, "He ordained twelve to be with Him, and to be sent out to preach, and to have authority to heal sicknesses and to cast out demons" (Mark 3:14–15). In this passage the master leader taught us how to conduct a meeting:

1. *He called the right people to the meeting.*
   There was no one in attendance who would not be directly accountable for his work in the kingdom. My guess is that

no disciple left the meeting feeling as though his time had been wasted.

2. *He taught by example.* The phrase "to be with Him" is evidence that Jesus was intentional about teaching the men by example. Some leaders don't want their followers to "be with" them. This type of positional leader wants to give orders for others to go and do. Jesus wanted to transfer His heart for leadership. Jesus wanted to know and be known.

3. *He imparted authority.* In another classic example of His leadership we see that Jesus gave authority to the men whom He would later hold accountable for their actions. Jesus was very specific about the actions that would follow the imparted authority.

    Low-level leaders demand productivity yet fail to give the proper authority to a team member to accomplish the stated goal. Yet Jesus knew authority must be coupled with accountability.

The most important observation about a meeting with Jesus is that teaching usually occurred. Jesus didn't seem to miss any opportunity to teach. Any meeting can be improved by a teacher.

There is one other participant love-driven leaders will want to consider. Twentieth-century preacher D. Martyn Lloyd-Jones asked a thought-provoking question in one of his sermons: "Is God in the midst of it?" We should ask ourselves a similar question: Is God in the middle of our meetings? Is He in our thoughts as we contemplate a decision? Is He in the front of our minds as we lead a training session?

We begin to answer these and other questions with our desire to invite the Lord in. Many of us want to be included in important meetings. We like to be invited to lunches and social experiences. Even if we cannot attend, we appreciate the invitation.

Leaders frequently fail to invite the Holy Spirit to weigh in on the next agenda item. We get busy and simply don't seek His presence. We go to others to seek counsel but fail to consult the Lord in prayer and study.

Brother Lawrence's classic book *The Practice of the Presence of God* offers this coaching:

> The most excellent method he had found of going to GOD, was that of doing our common business without any view of pleasing men [Gal. 1:10; Eph. 6:5–6], and (as far as we are capable) purely for the love of GOD.[1]

When we are practicing the presence of God, we have little concern for pleasing men. Our hearts become full of pleasing God. We lead for the love of God. We correct and train for the love of God. We lead as servants for the love of God. May the presence of the Lord be ever invited into our workdays. Lead us, Holy Spirit, that we may lead others into Your presence.

If You Forget Everything Else, Remember This

Scroll down in any leadership blog, and you will read about seven principles, four mandates, three proverbs, twelve characteristics, or any number of "leaders do this" lessons. I choose to offer one primary principle of leadership that Jesus taught:

> Remain in Me, as I also remain in you. As the branch cannot bear fruit by itself, unless it remains in the vine, neither can you, unless you remain in Me. I am the vine, you are the branches. He who remains in Me, and I in him, bears much fruit. For without Me you can do nothing.
>
> —JOHN 15:4–5

We cannot execute the golden rule of leadership in our own strength. Attempting to lead and serve others without Christ is malpractice. The branch is destined for the fire. This is what matters most: that we remain in Him. We can do nothing without Him. We certainly cannot love our teams without Him. There is no other foundation upon which a leader can build.

We must know Him, and we must remain in Him. When man begins to believe he is "all that," when he begins to believe his own press clippings, when he begins to believe the delusion that he can lead his team in his own strength, the leader withers like the branch.

> **Attempting to lead and serve others without Christ is malpractice.**

Consider the words of Christ: "If a man does not remain in Me, he is thrown out as a branch and withers. And they gather them and throw them into the fire, and they are burned" (John 15:6). Leaders who bear fruit labor to remain in Christ. They don't just accept Him as an authority in their lives; they trust Him for the daily manna to direct their teams. Fruit comes from the vine, not from the man who labors in the garden, no matter how hard he works. The healthiest vine is rooted and grounded in Jesus. We must remain in Him.

Social culture is overemphasized today. Social interaction is important, and more is better. But too much interaction can limit cognitive and creative skills. Time alone to reflect and solidify ideas is scarce today. My office has a constant influx of people. I have e-mails and texts to answer. I have production demands. I wailed yesterday afternoon that, "I don't have time to think."

If we aren't thinking, we are reacting rather than responding. A calculated response requires thinking! And if we don't have time to think, how do we have time to seek the Lord? I have purposeful prayer each morning, but my prayer time throughout the remainder of the day is often reduced to one-liners and, "Bless me, Lord." Is this God's best for my life? There is surely a call on the life of a leader to find a quiet place and be still before the Lord.

The popular worship song "The Heart of Worship" points to Jesus. Leading well is a form of worship. As we honor God with prayer and Bible study, we open our ears to hear how the Lord would have us lead with love.

The Heart of a Servant

I believe the closer I get to God, the better I will lead. It's easier to "die to self" when I remain near the cross. When I drift into being busy and "getting stuff done," I begin to lose the heart of a servant. Before long I'm singing a new song: "It's all about me; yes, it's all about me."

In the midst of those times it's hard for anyone to tell me I am leading myself and no one else. I may be managing others, but the servant-leader is out for a nap.

When I awake from such a slumber, I want to find the cross. I want to break my serving hiatus and lead others the way God expects me to lead. I know I'm serving as a love-driven leader when:

1. I am transparent; I have nothing to hide.

2. I have nothing to prove because God gives me confidence and removes my insecurities.

3. I don't fear man or losing anything because I know the Lord is my provider, and I'm free to serve Him.

4. I don't want anything. My needs are met, and I want time to be alone with God.

5. I inspire others. It's highly unlikely that I could ever inspire anyone while being self-serving. Self-serving leadership is accompanied by a distinct odor.

6. I don't need to be right because I know the truth always appears. Light reveals what is hidden in the dark.

7. I don't have to be heard because my actions tell the best story. I know that everything I do should point to the cross.

"Foot washing" is often used as a metaphor for servant leadership. In this day the act is not so difficult or humbling. It's not as relevant as when Jesus taught it. Today there are more humbling and significant ways to serve than to wash someone's feet. What is your modern-day-equivalent service? For me it starts with leaving my smartphone on my desk so I can stay attuned to the needs of others. Servant-leaders practice their serve.

My execution of the golden rule of leadership is demonstrated with sustained, consistent action on behalf of others. The golden rule is multiplied when it is taught, modeled, and copied by the team I lead. But it begins with my personal devotion in the time I spend alone with Jesus.

As with most things we must be intentional about finding time to be alone—alone without an umbilical connection to electronic engagement. I confess my time alone is too often used to catch up on social media, texts, and anything else my phone serves up. When Jesus went to His desert place to pray, He found true solitude. I believe He wants us to do likewise. Only when we spend time alone with Him will we be prepared to lead like Jesus.

Love-Driven Leader
Truths to Remember

- Effective leaders do more than the minimum.

- At the core of leader love is submission to the authority of Christ. That means we must understand how Christ led and how the Holy Spirit is leading us.

- Love-driven leaders care more about being principled than being liked.

- The Lord wants to be in the middle of our meetings.

- Leaders who bear fruit labor to remain in Christ. Fruit comes from the vine, not from the laborer.

- Servant-leaders practice their serve.

Chapter 13

LEADERSHIP LESSONS
FROM THE MOUNT

THE SERMON ON the Mount has often been called "The Constitution of the Kingdom," but it could also be called "A Constitution for Leader Love." From the Beatitudes to Jesus's teachings about anger, prayer, fasting, money, cares, and anxieties, Matthew 5, 6, and 7 help leaders who embrace these truths renew their minds and demonstrate the love of Christ.

Let's review a familiar passage, Matthew 5:3–10:

> Blessed are the poor in spirit, for theirs is the kingdom of heaven. Blessed are those who mourn, for they shall be comforted. Blessed are the meek, for they shall inherit the earth. Blessed are those who hunger and thirst for righteousness, for they shall be filled. Blessed are the merciful, for they shall obtain mercy. Blessed are the pure in heart, for they shall see God. Blessed are the peacemakers, for they shall be called the sons of God. Blessed are those who

are persecuted for righteousness' sake, for theirs
is the kingdom of heaven.

This is our standard as Christians, but more is
required of leaders. Leaders must certainly model this
teaching but also find ways to expand its directive and
apply it to modern situations in the church, in the marketplace, and most certainly on the home front. Let's
explore some of the leadership lessons that can be
found in the Sermon on the Mount.

Love Leaders
Depend on God

It may sound contrary—and it *is* contrary—to the
world's ways, but rich leadership is birthed in poverty
of spirit. When Jesus said, "Blessed are the poor in
spirit," He wasn't speaking of being poor from a financial perspective but being needy from a spiritual perspective. The Greek word for *poverty* in Matthew 5:3 is
ptōchos. According to *The KJV New Testament Greek
Lexicon*, *ptōchos* means "begging, needy, and powerless
to accomplish an end."[1] This is in line with what Jesus
said: "For without Me you can do nothing" (John 15:5).

Success tends to breed independence of God, and
when we begin to feel that independence, our cries to
Him become less frequent. Perhaps the best leaders are
those who understand that apart from Christ we can't

lead rightly. These leaders understand their utter dependence on God to love well and to lead well—to do anything and everything well—and take Jesus's advice to remain in Him so they can bear much fruit (John 15:5).

The poor in spirit remain dependent on God, particularly in the midst of success. It seems to me that the essence of living and leading as one poor in spirit is to never believe that God's gifts are to be used for personal gain. The gifts God gave me are to be used to help others. I'm not wearing a shirt with a big *S* on my chest. I want to remain as soft clay on the potter's wheel, and that comes from a revelation of John 15:5.

> **Perhaps the best leaders are those who understand that apart from Christ we can't lead rightly.**

Leaders who are poor in spirit don't make hasty decisions. They wait upon the Lord for direction. They do as Solomon suggests: "Trust in the LORD with all your heart, and lean not on your own understanding; in all your ways acknowledge Him, and He will direct your paths" (Prov. 3:5–6). This is not always easy to do in a fast-paced, information-driven society, but it produces outcomes laced with love. Leaders who are poor in spirit spend time on their knees so they can see what the Father is doing and act accordingly.

Love Leaders Mourn
With Those Who Mourn

I believe the Lord's message about mourners is of great importance to leaders. We are to mourn when we see ourselves and others behave like the carnally minded. Repentance is comforting. I know when I err toward others and bellow with the strength of man, I miss God's favor and comfort.

When I am less than God wants me to be, I want to run to Him for restoration with a cry like David's: "Search me, O God, and know my heart: try me, and know my thoughts: and see if there be any wicked way in me, and lead me in the way everlasting" (Ps. 139:23–24, KJV). God's love draws us to mourn our mistakes and seek forgiveness.

When we observe our team members doing the wrong things for wrong reasons, we may have a tendency to rare up in strength and demand correction. When mistakes are made, loving leaders confront and teach. A leader's desire should be to help the team member find his own way to repair a problem. My job as a leader is not to make a worker mourn. We want the worker to mourn on her own and seek favor from the Lord. We can even mourn with the person.

Consider Paul's reflection of his loving correction to the church at Corinth, where members were engaging in sexual sin:

Though I caused you sorrow by my letter, I do not regret it, though I did regret it. For I perceive that this same letter has caused you sorrow, though only for a while. Now I rejoice, not that you were made sorrowful, but that your sorrow led to repentance. For you were made sorrowful in a godly way, that you might not suffer loss in any way through us. Godly sorrow produces repentance that leads to salvation and brings no regret, but the sorrow of the world produces death. For observe this very thing, which you sorrowed in a godly way: What carefulness it produced in you, what vindication of yourselves, what indignation, what fear, what intense desire, what zeal, what avenging of wrong! In all things you have proven yourselves to be innocent in this matter. So though I wrote to you, I did it not because of him who had done the wrong, nor because of him who suffered wrong, but that our care for you in the sight of God might be evident to you. Therefore we were comforted in your comfort.

—2 CORINTHIANS 7:8–13

Joy comes in the mourning. When I feel confronted by the Holy Spirit, I feel as if He has asked me questions, just as the Lord has done throughout Scripture:

- 1 Kings 19:9: "Why are you here, Elijah?"

- Mark 8:29: "Who do you say that I am, [Peter]?"

- Mark 9:33: "[Disciples,] what was it that you disputed among yourselves on the way?"

The Lord knows the answer to every question He asks before He asks it. It is my free moral agency to confess my weakness and seek His strength. Comfort comes to us when we cry out for His strength.

Love Leaders Seek Meekness (Not Weakness)

Solomon so plainly said, "Pride goes before destruction, and a haughty spirit before a fall" (Prov. 16:18). Strong and highly effective leaders walk on a slippery slope. Pride can attack a leader more quickly than competitive forces.

Loving leaders seek meekness. Meekness is not weakness. You may have heard meekness defined as strength under control. That is a good way to define it. Jesus described Himself as meek, and He was anything but weak.

Jesus said, "Come to Me, all you who labor and are heavily burdened, and I will give you rest. Take My yoke upon you, and learn from Me. For I am meek and lowly in heart, and you will find rest for your souls. For My yoke is easy, and My burden is light" (Matt. 11:28–30). According to *The KJV New Testament Greek Lexicon*, the word Jesus used to describe Himself—*praos*—means "gentle, mild, meek."[2] It comes from a root word that means "mildness of disposition, gentleness of spirit, meekness."[3]

I remember a leader told me once not to believe my press clippings. He was telling me not to get too full of myself based on what others tell me. Many great preachers, such as healing evangelist Kathryn Kuhlman, would not read letters of praise or criticism because they sought to be concerned only with what God said and thought about them.

I am constantly reminded to stay low as I think big. I heard evangelist Oral Roberts tell others that his mother regularly reminded him to stay below himself. I can only imagine how people with a gift of healing must struggle not to think too highly of themselves. But if they are wise, they know the power doesn't come from them but from God. The same is true of us as leaders. The strength and wisdom to lead our teams comes from the Lord.

Love Leaders Hunger and Thirst for Righteousness

Love-driven leaders hunger and thirst after righteousness. But what is righteousness? Let's start with what it is not—self-righteousness. A self-righteous leader is not a meek leader. The self-righteous leader is a proud and haughty leader. The self-righteous leader is "narrow-mindedly moralistic," to quote one of Merriam-Webster's definitions of the term.[4]

That dictionary also defines *self-righteous* as being "convinced of one's own righteousness especially in contrast with the actions and beliefs of others."[5] Self-righteous leaders think they are always right, which limits the creativity of their teams, stifles new ideas, and casts intimidation on those around them. If love is present in this leadership style, it's heavily camouflaged.

By position we are the righteousness of God in Christ Jesus (2 Cor. 5:21). But sometimes our behavior as leaders—especially if we have type A personalities—does not demonstrate God's righteousness. One definition of *righteousness* comes from Genesis 15:6: "Then Abram believed in (affirmed, trusted in, relied on, remained steadfast to) the LORD; and He counted (credited) it to him as righteousness (doing right in regard to God and man)" (AMP). God cares about how we treat people. Jesus said, "By this all men will know that you are My disciples, if you have love for one another" (John

13:35). Love is not self-righteous. Leader love seeks to do right by God and man. We cannot do wrong by men and think we're doing right by God, but our flesh wars with the Spirit, and the unrighteous work of the flesh will manifest if we do not, as Paul said, seek to die daily (1 Cor. 15:31).

> **Self-righteous leaders think they are always right, which limits the creativity of their teams, stifles new ideas, and casts intimidation on those around them.**

Love-driven leaders literally hunger and thirst to show forth the righteousness of God and the fruit of the Spirit. One definition of the Greek word translated *hunger* in Matthew 5:6 is a metaphor: "to crave ardently, to seek with eager desire."[6] This is a strong picture of how fervent a leader should be in seeking the answer to "What would Jesus do?" in every situation.

Likewise the Greek word translated "thirst" in Matthew 5:6 paints a striking picture. It means "to suffer thirst, suffer from thirst" and figuratively "those who are said to thirst who painfully feel their want of, and eagerly long for, those things by which the soul is refreshed, supported, strengthened."[7] Love-driven leaders suffer when they don't reflect the righteousness of Christ and seek to reconcile situations to the glory of God.

Love Leaders Show Forth God's Mercy

James teaches us "mercy triumphs over judgment" (James 2:13). Certainly he learned this from his half brother Jesus. Matthew 7 opens with a stern warning about judgment. Leader love doesn't judge in a wrong spirit. It doesn't assume. It discerns, disciplines, and decides, but it does not make unrighteous judgments.

Let's review Jesus's warning:

> Judge not, that you be not judged. For with what judgment you judge, you will be judged. And with the measure you use, it will be measured again for you. And why do you see the speck that is in your brother's eye, but do not consider the plank that is in your own eye? Or how will you say to your brother, "Let me pull the speck out of your eye," when a log is in your own eye? You hypocrite! First take the plank out of your own eye, and then you will see clearly to take the speck out of your brother's eye.
>
> —MATTHEW 7:1–5

I have to be careful how I speak to my golden retriever. She can take offense even when I meant the words for good. I say something like, "No more biscuits," in my alpha dog voice, and her ears drop, her tail stops wagging, and she finds a place to curl up and take a nap. Bad leader!

Effective leaders are careful to observe the impact of their tone of voice as well as their specific word choice. Whether intentional or accidental, an inattentive leader can create a feeling of guilt within her team.

My observation is that many leaders use guilt as a weapon. Perhaps leaders who guilt their teams into compliance believe if they can make a person feel bad enough about their performance, the worker will jump to his feet with a strong desire to do better. If I understand the embedded logic, this type of leadership suggests, "Make a person or a team feel bad, and they will work better." How inspiring! Guilt trips generally have the opposite effect.

> **Effective leaders are careful to observe the impact of their tone of voice as well as their specific word choice.**

206

Love Leaders Pursue Purity of Heart

Jesus called the pure in heart blessed. Purity of heart has to do with our motives. Love-driven leaders are as motivated to build people as they are to build a business. You may have heard the legendary Zig Ziglar's quote "You don't build a business—you build people—and then people build the business."[8] That quote can also apply to your church, your family, and your life. Build yourself; build the people around you. God will then use you and others to build what He wants to build—in, through, and around you.

Take some time to consider your motives. Love-driven leaders pursue success, but not at the expense of the people around them. Love-driven leaders pursue excellence, but not above being ambassadors for Christ in their conduct. Love-driven leaders are motivated ultimately by a desire to glorify God. The apostle Paul reminds us of this in three passages of Scripture that help ground us in the pursuit of pure motives:

> And whatever you do, do it heartily, as for the Lord and not for men, knowing that from the Lord you will receive the reward of the inheritance. For you serve the Lord Christ.
>
> —Colossians 3:23–24

Therefore, whether you eat, or drink, or whatever you do, do it all to the glory of God.

—1 Corinthians 10:31

Not serving when eyes are on you, but as pleasing men as the servants of Christ, doing the will of God from the heart, with good will doing service, as to the Lord, and not to men, knowing that whatever good thing any man does, he will receive the same from the Lord.

—Ephesians 6:6–8

Likewise love-driven leaders are not motivated solely by the bottom line. Money is always a concern in this world, but when money becomes our primary driver as leaders, we fail in love because we've muddied the waters of our hearts. Jesus plainly said, "No one can serve two masters. For either he will hate the one and love the other, or else he will hold to the one and despise the other. You cannot serve God and money" (Matt. 6:24).

Remember, "the love of money is the root of all evil" (1 Tim. 6:10). The love of people has eternal rewards beyond top-line sales, church-membership stats, or any other metric.

Love Leaders Make Peace
Everywhere They Go

The peacemakers are blessed. As much as we crave to operate in wisdom and spiritual gifts, we should crave to operate in peace. Love-driven leaders are lovers of peace. The Bible tells us to be at peace with all people, as much as it depends on us (Rom. 12:18).

It's not always easy to walk in peace when you work in a pressure cooker of deadlines—and we know the enemy wants to steal our peace at every turn. That's why we must be intentional to put on our shoes of peace, one element of God's armor listed in Ephesians 6. We can choose to ask for God's grace to walk in peace when deadlines are looming, when clients are cranky, when employees are out sick and leave a gap in the works, or when we are overstressed and overwhelmed by natural circumstances of life.

Once we're walking in peace, we can seek to be peacemakers with others, resolving conflicts with those around us. There aren't many leaders of organizations who haven't experienced division in their midst. I learned early in my career that division is a common strategy of the enemy. It seems to me that spiritual unity is rare. Paul taught us to expect dividers and division.

To keep division out of your midst and establish a culture of peace, remain focused on spiritual matters. Lead with your feet firmly planted in godly principles.

Self-preservation is one thing, but the health of the flock cannot be forgotten. When we get caught up in "why are they doing this to me?" pity parties, it's easy to lose focus on how the dissenters will affect the overall organization.

Wolves will come. Some leaders simply deny the existence of wolves. They fail to see and understand the impact of cancer cells. "Watch and pray" is a powerful admonition from the Lord. We can nip division in the bud and broker peace quickly if we discern the enemy's work to rob us of peace at the onset. During a season of division the love-driven leader will remain focused on his own submission to the Lord. Conflict resolution schema may or may not be effective. As love-inspired leaders our overarching goal is to achieve peace and unity.

Love Leaders
Accept Persecution

Love leaders may experience persecution at times—persecution from competitors, persecution from colleagues, persecution from the wicked one, and even self-persecution when we don't rise up to the level of excellence we hope for ourselves. The latter is called condemnation.

Love leaders pray for those who persecute them and move in the opposite spirit. Love-driven leaders turn the other cheek, walk the extra mile, and give up their cloak for the sake of obeying the Lord. That doesn't mean you're called to be a doormat, but rather an example of Christ. Jesus and the apostles were persecuted, yet they kept their eyes on the prize. Love-driven leaders do the same.

Love Leaders Seek Excellence, Not Perfection

Remember, we are not seeking perfection. Perfection is a lofty goal. It also limits our output. Leaders who seek perfection are rarely satisfied, often disappointed, and generally less productive. Perfectionists simply do not get as much done as leaders who accept excellence as their goal. Excellence is also difficult to achieve, but at least excellence is attainable. As we lead our teams to excellence, we set a course built upon realistic expectations.

This powerful question is a barometer of excellence: "Can we improve this project without adding costs or resources?" It's not that difficult to observe a project and see room for improvement. Effective leaders look for improvement with an eye on all elements of cost:

- Finances: What is the absolute cost for each milestone of excellence? Apply the concept of marginal utility—the benefit or satisfaction derived from consuming a product—to an analysis of excellence.

- Human capital: How will our pursuit of an increment affect our people? Is the next notch worth burning midnight oil and human stress?

- Opportunity cost: What won't we be working on while we inch this project further toward perfection?

- Return on investment (ROI): What is the ROI of the pursuit of excellence? Considering the factors listed previously may go a long way toward helping make this assessment.

Work is excellent when we have done all we can do with what we have been given. The role of a leader is to make sure we have done all and that having done all, we stand in faith.

Wise Leaders Love

The Sermon on the Mount ends with a promise and a warning that leaders would do well to heed. This is especially poignant considering the axiom "everything rises and falls on leadership." Consider Christ's words in Matthew 7:24–27:

Whoever hears these sayings of Mine and does them, I will liken him to a wise man who built his house on a rock. And the rain descended, the floods came, and the winds blew and beat on that house. And it did not fall, for it was founded a rock. And every one who hears these sayings of Mine and does not do them will be likened to a foolish man who built his house on the sand. And the rain descended, the floods came, and the winds blew and beat on that house. And it fell. And its fall was great.

With every thought, word, and action love-driven leaders are building their lives, families, ministries, businesses, employees, and volunteers on a rock. When the winds of adversity blow, love will lead the way through. By contrast, leaders who lead with fear may get short-term results, but when hard times come, the sheep will scatter because they don't trust the shepherd.

The love of God is present in every word of this sermon. We hear God's will through the words of Jesus. The Beatitudes remind us of the ideal condition of our hearts. As we lead with the heart of God, we are ever reaching beyond our own beliefs and opinions to a higher standard, the Word of God and the example of Christ.

Love-Driven Leader
Truths to Remember

- The best leaders are those who understand that apart from Christ they can't lead rightly.

- Love-driven leaders seek to do right by God and man. They cannot do wrong by men and think they're doing right by God.

- Effective leaders are careful to observe the impact of their tone of voice as well as their specific word choice.

- As love-inspired leaders our overarching goal is to achieve peace and unity.

- Leaders who seek perfection are rarely satisfied, often disappointed, and generally less productive. Perfectionists simply do not get as much done as leaders who accept excellence as their goal.

Conclusion

LET LOVE REMAIN

Those who write about leadership seem dedicated to defining the crown of effective leadership as "leaving a legacy." Some writers suggest five, seven, or ten levels of leadership progression, with the last being legacy leadership.

The dangling carrot for a leader is to do something, build something, or say a lot of somethings that outlast a lifetime. Maybe this explains why I like to see my quotes on Twitter enveloped in a meme. I can convince myself that my words will forever mark the Twitterverse.

I searched the Bible for the *l* word and found nothing in most translations. A few versions, including the Modern English Version, include the word in this one verse: "The wise will inherit glory, but shame will be the legacy of fools" (Prov. 3:35).

I can best understand the word *legacy* through a synonym such as an inheritance or gift of money or property. But it seems leadership writers are referring to something more.

Some suggest that philosophers left a legacy in their manner of thinking out loud. (And those ancient philosophers had nary a tweet among them.) And Billy Graham once said this about legacy: "Our days are numbered. One of the primary goals in our lives should be to prepare for our last day. The legacy we leave is not just in our possessions, but in the quality of our lives. What preparations should we be making now? The greatest waste in all our earth, which cannot be recycled or reclaimed, is our waste of the time God has given us each day."[1]

These are all useful ways of understanding legacy, but do they describe the legacy of a love-driven leader?

A Legacy of Faithfulness

A good friend of mine suggested I consider the Bible's "hall of faith" to gain an understanding of legacy. Hebrews 11 is peppered with legacy imprints. The Book of Hebrews is pastoral in nature, and it seems to be written to encourage and edify.

In chapter 11 the author forms a message arc around the importance of faith in our Christian walk. After making an opening statement on faith, he references the lives of men and women who modeled faith.

Apparently this is how their legacy was established—in faith. And we know faith works through love (Gal. 5:6).

The chapter begins:

> Now faith is the substance of things hoped for, the evidence of things not seen. For by it the men of old obtained a good report. By faith we understand that the universe was framed by the word of God, so that things that are seen were not made out of things which are visible. By faith Abel offered to God a more excellent sacrifice than Cain offered. Through this he was approved as righteous, with God testifying concerning his gifts. He still speaks through his faith, though he is dead.
>
> —Hebrews 11:1–4

If you hope to leave a "good report"—a strong legacy—walking in faith, which works through love, is your aim. By faith Abel demonstrated his love to God through his obedience and sacrifice, and his faith still speaks volumes to this day. As we learned in the pages of this book, love-driven leaders sacrifice.

Hebrews 11 goes on to say:

> By faith Enoch was taken to heaven so that he would not see death. He was not found, because God took him away. For before he was taken, he

had this commendation, that he pleased God. And without faith it is impossible to please God, for he who comes to God must believe that He exists and that He is a rewarder of those who diligently seek Him.

—HEBREWS 11:5–6

The Bible tells us Enoch walked with God for 300 years (Gen. 5:22). Can you imagine? All told, he lived 365 years and never tasted death. His legacy is that he pleased God. I could live with that! Love-driven leaders seek to please God and are quick to repent when they don't.

It seems Enoch's legacy of faithfulness to God influenced future generations. His grandson Noah also made the hall of faith.

By faith Noah, being divinely warned about things not yet seen, moved with godly fear, prepared an ark to save his family, by which he condemned the world and became an heir of the righteousness that comes by faith.

—HEBREWS 11:7

Noah feared the Lord and demonstrated a righteousness earned not by works but by faith. Noah's legacy is obedience in the face of what looked ridiculous—and his obedience essentially saved the human race. As I have said in this book, love-driven leaders take risks.

We see this also in the life of Abraham:

> By faith Abraham obeyed when he was called to go out into a place which he would later receive as an inheritance. He went out not knowing where he was going. By faith he dwelt in the promised land, as in a foreign land, dwelling in tents with Isaac and Jacob, the heirs of the same promise, for he was looking for a city which has foundations, whose builder and maker is God. By faith Sarah herself also received the ability to conceive seed, and she bore a child when she was past the age, because she judged Him faithful who had promised. Therefore from one man, who was as good as dead, sprang so many, a multitude as the stars of the sky and innumerable as the sand by the seashore.
>
> —Hebrews 11:8–12

Abraham's legacy is marked by blind faith. He truly walked by faith and not by sight. He was a friend of God's (James 2:23). His wife Sarah stood with him. Abraham's legacy blesses us today, as the Bible tells us, "Christ has redeemed us from the curse of the law by being made a curse for us—as it is written, 'Cursed is everyone who hangs on a tree'—so that the blessing of

Abraham might come on the Gentiles through Jesus Christ, that we might receive the promise of the Spirit through faith" (Gal. 3:13–14).

Again, in Abraham we see a legacy of faithfulness that influenced generations.

> By faith Isaac blessed Jacob and Esau concerning things to come. By faith Jacob, when he was dying, blessed each of the sons of Joseph and worshipped while leaning on the top of his staff. By faith Joseph, when he was dying, mentioned the exodus of the children of Israel and gave instructions concerning his bones....By faith the walls of Jericho fell down after they were encircled for seven days. By faith the prostitute Rahab, when she received the spies with peace, did not perish with those who did not believe.
> —HEBREWS 11:20–22, 30–31

The writer of Hebrews also mentions "Gideon, Barak, Samson, Jephthah, of David and Samuel and the prophets, who through faith subdued kingdoms, administered justice, obtained promises, stopped the mouths of lions, quenched the violence of fire, escaped the edge of the sword, out of weakness were made strong, became valiant in fighting, and turned the armies of foreign enemies to flight" (Heb. 11:32–34).

Love-driven leadership is moved by faith, which

works through love. Even when you spy out the land and it looks as if the giants are too great for you, you can choose to see through the eyes of faith, as Joshua and Caleb did (Num. 13). Love-driven leadership seeks the Lord, finds confidence in Him, and executes His vision in His timing and in His way for His glory. And it takes great faith, which works through love.

A Legacy of Love

Indeed, faith seems to be interwoven with legacy. Leaders with little faith probably do not leave a legacy. So consider this question: When you make decisions, do you consider how your choices will impact your legacy? Should you?

We know politicians wring their hands over the legacies they will leave. But do CEOs of Fortune 500 companies plan trips to exotic locations to create legacy plans? Do pastors do such a thing?

To me thinking about my legacy is egomaniacal. Whatever I have said and done by the end of my life will speak for itself. If I have followed the Holy Spirit, I should have no concerns about what remains after my body does not. A leader who leaves a strong legacy has died to self. Our mission as leaders is to live through Christ and take up our crosses daily.

> **When you make decisions, do
> you consider how your choices
> will impact your legacy?**

I will give an account of my legacy on that great and glorious day. And so will you. Let us remember the words of Paul the apostle in 1 Corinthians 13 once again because I believe the best way to leave a lasting legacy is to lead with love:

> If I speak with the tongues of men and of angels, and have not love, I have become as sounding brass or a clanging cymbal. If I have the gift of prophecy, and understand all mysteries and all knowledge, and if I have all faith, so that I could remove mountains, and have not love, I am nothing. If I give all my goods to feed the poor, and if I give my body to be burned, and have not love, it profits me nothing.
>
> Love suffers long and is kind; love envies not; love flaunts not itself and is not puffed up, does not behave itself improperly, seeks not its own, is not easily provoked, thinks no evil; rejoices not in iniquity, but rejoices in the truth; bears all things, believes all things, hopes all things, and endures all things.
>
> Love never fails. But if there are prophecies,

they shall fail; if there are tongues, they shall cease; and if there is knowledge, it shall vanish. For we know in part, and we prophesy in part. But when that which is perfect comes, then that which is imperfect shall pass away. When I was a child, I spoke as a child, I understood as a child, and I thought as a child. But when I became a man, I put away childish things. For now we see as through a glass, dimly, but then, face to face. Now I know in part, but then I shall know, even as I also am known.

So now abide faith, hope, and love, these three. But the greatest of these is love.

The teams we lead will remember us not by profits earned or buildings built. We will be remembered by the love we have demonstrated. When I am gone, I pray that love will remain.

NOTES

Chapter 1
The Case for Love

1. *Merriam-Webster's Collegiate Dictionary*, eleventh edition (Springfield, MA: Merriam-Webster Inc., 2003), s.v. "potential."

Chapter 2
The Faith of a Leader

1. Jonathan Cahn, *The Book of Mysteries* (Lake Mary, FL: Charisma House, 2016), 27.

2. Bryan Chapell with Kathy Chapell, *Each for the Other: Marriage as It's Meant to Be* (Grand Rapids, MI: Baker Books, 1998), 15.

Chapter 3
Relationships Precede Influence

1. Theory X is an authoritarian style in which "the emphasis is on 'productivity, on the concept of a fair day's work, on the evils of feather-bedding and restriction of output, on rewards for performance...[it] reflects an underlying belief that management must counteract an inherent human tendency to avoid work.'" See "Theories X and Y," *The Economist*, October 6, 2008, accessed April 5, 2017, http://www.economist.com/node/12370445.

2. *Merriam-Webster's Collegiate Dictionary*, s.v. "supplant."

Chapter 4
Managing Entropy

1. *Merriam-Webster's Collegiate Dictionary*, s.v. "entropy."

Chapter 5
Loving Through a Crisis

1. *The Andy Griffith Show*, "One-Punch Opie," aired December 31, 1962, clip viewed at https://www.youtube .com/watch?v=gU5iLiEySyk.

Chapter 6
Leaders Act and Keep Acting

1. Oswald Chambers, "Take the Initiative," *My Utmost for His Highest*, accessed January 26, 2017, https://utmost .org/take-the-initiative/.

Chapter 8
Rooted in Prayer

1. Rodney Fry, "The Tender Heart of a Tough Leader," Sermon Central, August 5, 2007, accessed April 5, 2017, http://www.sermoncentral.com/sermons/the-tender-heart -of-a-tough-leader-rodney-fry-sermon-on-leadership -general-110153?page=2; "Why Prayer Should Precede All You Do," BCNN1, October 29, 2015, accessed April 5, 2017, http://blackchristiannews.tumblr.com/tagged/A.J.-Gordon.

2. Jay Maeder, "The Guy in the Sky Shipwreck Kelly," *New York Daily News*, September 19, 1999, accessed April 5,

2017, http://www.nydailynews.com/archives/news/guy-sky-shipwreck-kelly-article-1.850977.

3. *Encyclopaedia Britannica Online*, s.v. "Saint Simeon Stylites," accessed April 5, 2017, https://www.britannica.com/biography/Saint-Simeon-Stylites; *Encyclopaedia Britannica Online*, s.v. "Stylite," accessed April 5, 2017, https://www.britannica.com/topic/stylite.

4. *Merriam-Webster's Collegiate Dictionary*, s.v. "stylite."

5. *Encyclopaedia Britannica Online*, s.v. "Saint Simeon Stylites."

Chapter 10
Leaders Love a Fishbowl

1. "George S. Patton Quotes," Brainy Quote, accessed April 7, 2017, https://www.brainyquote.com/quotes/quotes/g/georgespa159766.html.

2. James Clear, "Vince Lombardi on the Hidden Power of Mastering the Fundamentals," *The Huffington Post*, February 29, 2016, accessed April 7, 2017, http://www.huffingtonpost.com/james-clear/vince-lombardi-on-the-hid_b_9306782.html.

Chapter 11
The Presence of Love

1. A. W. Tozer, *The Pursuit of God* (Bloomington, MN: Bethany House, 2013).

2. "Our History," Gordon Ramsay Restaurants, accessed April 7, 2017, https://www.gordonramsayrestaurants.com/careers/about/.

3. Peter Drucker and Isao Nakauchi, *Drucker on Asia* (New York: Routledge, 1997), 108–109.

4. Ibid.

5. Kenneth Blanchard and Spencer Johnson, *The One Minute Manager* (William Morrow & Co., 1982).

Chapter 12
The Golden Rule of Leadership

1. Brother Lawrence, *The Practice of the Presence of God*, Project Gutenberg, accessed April 7, 2017, http://www.gutenberg.org/cache/epub/13871/pg13871-images.html.

Chapter 13
Leadership Lessons From the Mount

1. *The KJV New Testament Greek Lexicon*, s.v. "*ptochos*," accessed April 7, 2017, http://www.biblestudytools.com/lexicons/greek/kjv/ptochos.html.

2. *The KJV New Testament Greek Lexicon*, s.v. "*praos*," accessed April 7, 2017, http://www.biblestudytools.com/lexicons/greek/kjv/praos.html.

3. *The KJV New Testament Greek Lexicon*, s.v. "*praus*," accessed April 7, 2017, http://www.biblestudytools.com/lexicons/greek/kjv/praus.html.

4. *Merriam-Webster's Collegiate Dictionary*, s.v. "self-righteous."

5. Ibid.

6. *The KJV New Testament Greek Lexicon*, s.v. "*peinao*," accessed April 7, 2017, http://www.biblestudytools.com/lexicons/greek/kjv/peinao.html.

7. *The KJV New Testament Greek Lexicon*, s.v. "*dipsao*," accessed April 7, 2017, http://www.biblestudytools.com/lexicons/greek/kjv/dipsao.html.

8. Kim Synder, "People Builders," ZigZiglar.com, October 22, 2015, accessed April 7, 2017, https://www.ziglar.com/quotes/business-people/.

Conclusion
Let Love Remain

1. Quoted by John Maxwell in *Talent Is Never Enough* (Nashville, TN: Thomas Nelson, 2007), 140–141.

CONNECT WITH US!